Officer Safety Redefined

Dr. Laura King

Published by Mental Dominion Publishing, 2020.

The characters and events portrayed in this book are fictitious. Any similarity to real persons, living or dead, is coincidental and not intended by the author.

No part of this book may be reproduced, or stored in a retrieval system, or transmitted in any form or by any means, electronic, mechanical, photocopying, recording, or otherwise, without express written permission of the publisher.

While every precaution has been taken in the preparation of this book, the publisher assumes no responsibility for errors or omissions, or for damages resulting from the use of the information contained herein.

This book is dedicated to my parents;
Glenn and Linda Virgils.
Your unconditional love and support has allowed me to find the courage to pursue my dreams.
I would not be who I am today without you.

ISBN: 978-1735564401

Mental Dominion Publishing

Printed in the United States of America

Copyright © 2020 Laura LV King All rights reserved

Chapter 1: The Officer Wellness Revolution

"We need a revolution every 200 years..."
– Ben Franklin

- Understand all the components that contribute to comprehensive officer safety
- Explain how the psychological threats regularly encountered by police officers are impacting our mental state
- Discover the research that shows officers have more control of their physical health than they may believe

Be the Change

Something in law enforcement must change. All of us who have signed on to work as part of this noble profession are aware of how dangerous police work can be. The necessity to intervene in emergency situations combined with the unpredictable nature of the street create a lot of unknowns for police. Add to that civil unrest, violent offenders and the rampant abuse of controlled substances in our society and we know it is only a matter of time before we encounter a situation that could be a real threat to our safety. Still, each year thousands of new recruits join our team despite these realities. In order to keep new and experienced officers as safe as possible, we have created a comprehensive plan to prepare our police for the dangers they almost certainly will encounter.

We train for this. We go to the academy, we run scenarios, we learn defensive tactics and wear equipment designed to protect us from these officer safety threats. This training continues year in and year out. Despite all these protective efforts, the number of officers hurt and/or killed in the line of duty continues to grow. This is because law enforcement remains an inherently dangerous profession. There are so many things that training just cannot control. The dangers encountered on the street are only part of the story. There are other dangers lurking in the dark. These issues are little discussed and trained for even more infrequently. Truth be told, when it comes to matters of officer safety, these issues are just as dangerous as an armed violent offender.

Across the nation, agencies proclaim that matters of officer safety are amongst their top priorities. Despite this, officers often feel their departments are more concerned with the number of tickets they write than the larger issues revolving around officer safety. This is because most of law enforcement's daily focus is often on operational matters. It is time we work cooperatively to find a way to ensure the foundational issues that create a healthy police culture are invested in, cultivated and allowed to flourish. This needs to occur in small and large agencies alike. In order to accomplish this, we need to change the narrative surrounding officer safety.

In 1838, Boston established the first full time American police force. In those days, officer wellness was likely not something actively discussed. Life was different. Those were simpler times and police did not see nearly the same amount of violence and moral compromise in society as officers today are exposed to. As we near the 200-year anniversary of law enforcement in America, we must look at our profession and see if we have made a responsible effort to adjust with the times, or if there are any areas in our professional landscape in need of radical change. When we do this, we see officer safety issues, specifically the psychological threats of our profession, as the most noticeable area where law enforcement is failing to meet the needs of our men and women in uniform.

Proactively addressing the psychological threats of our profession can seem overwhelming at first. This causes well intentioned people to back away from the issue and find an easier task to manage. This issue can be addressed with the same approach as any other major area of concern. The best strategy to solving this problem is to break the issue into bite-size pieces. This is what this book is intended to do. Help police officers across the nation accept personal responsibility for matters of officer safety. It is also written to empower each of us to prepare for and meet the psychological threats of the law enforcement profession. Each of us needs to take responsibility to find the solutions to comprehensive wellness that our profession has failed to provide us with. We need to take the "Ghandi" approach to officer wellness. We need to be the change…

Own Your Safety

To ensure that officer safety is a top foundational priority that we build our careers upon, each of us must take personal responsibility for what we can control. Our agencies do have some level of responsibility for officer safety. I am not saying they don't. They hold responsibility for providing functional equipment, establishing responsible policies, and committing to training for their officers... to name just a few. These efforts are not enough to protect officers from the physical or psychological threats of this profession. Every officer who truly understands the importance of officer safety, knows individual effort is required to ensure they are safe on the street.

One of the largest areas of individual responsibility lies with taking action to prepare ourselves for the psychological dangers associated with a career in law enforcement. Most police agencies continue to limit their commitment to officer safety exclusively to preparing their officers for the physical safety threats officers encounter on the street. Dr. Kevin Gilmartin, almost 20 years ago, challenged the law enforcement profession to start focusing on psychological safety threats with the same intensity as the physical safety threats facing officers (Gilmartin, 2002). Despite the convincing call to action in his *Emotional Survival for Law Enforcement* presented almost two decades ago, little has changed.

It is time we stop relying on our agencies to provide for our officer safety needs and realize we hold the ultimate responsibility for our own personal safety. At times, we become so frustrated with our agencies apparent lack of commitment to our well-being that we give up. When that happens, we begin to become complacent. In frustration, many law enforcement professionals take on the attitude that if officer wellness was truly an officer safety issue, the agency would be providing its officers with the tools necessary (money, time, and training) to take care of the essential safety needs. This attitude is dangerous and has helped to create the problem we are currently facing.

If we accept it is our agencies responsibility to ensure our safety, we stop engaging in a proactive way. This is when our daily habits can become compromised. Complacency kills: every police officer knows this. It is a fundamental mantra of our profession. What we have failed to understand is this is not only true when it comes to the threats of the street, but also of our personal well-being. We need to find a way to incorporate habits designed to protect us against both the physical *and* psychological threats of our profession to truly ensure our safety.

Yes, complacency kills. It kills in many ways. Failure to practice good tactics can compromise our safety on a call or traffic stop. Failure to care for our psychological wellness can also lead to significant officer safety threats. Depression, addiction, and suicide are amongst the most wide-spread examples of the impact of compromised mental wellness. In fact, we lose more officers to suicide each year than we do to all line of duty deaths combined. This needs to change. Something must be done. We will discuss comprehensive action steps to protect mental wellness in depth later in this book.

Officer Safety and Physical Health

Failure to take responsibility for our physical health can also lead to serious issues that can compromise our safety in equally dangerous ways. To prove this point I would like to share a little-known reality of our profession with you. Heart disease is one of the leading causes of death for law enforcement professionals. While heart attacks account for only about 10% of line of duty deaths, if you add up the number of police professionals both on and off duty, who suffer heart attacks during the course of their career, those numbers are significantly higher (Kulbarsh, 2018). Heart disease is directly related to your physical fitness and the efforts you take to maintain it. Physical fitness is another important area that must become part of the new narrative surrounding officer safety.

As a profession and as a society we have been misinformed about heart disease and the amount of control we have over it. Many people mistakenly believe genetic predisposition is largely responsible for things like high blood pressure, high cholesterol, and cardiovascular disease. The time for using that as an excuse is over.

Modern research confirms that genetics have far less to do with disease than previously thought. In fact, research proves most health issues have only a 10-20% genetic link contributing to the development of disease (Greger, 2018). So why do things like high blood pressure or high cholesterol seem to run in families if they are not caused by genetics? The simple answer is they are connected to your daily habits and lifestyle choices, most of which are learned within your family and household environment.

Honored family recipes, traditions, and daily routines are all examples of how we develop habits that might be contributing to what we previously believed to be a genetic link. If you had parents who valued physical fitness and exercised regularly, you likely grew up modeling these behaviors and incorporating exercise into your life. If you had a family who engaged in more sedentary activities, such as playing cards or watching television, these are likely the types of activities you learned to enjoy. Both types of activities can have a place in a healthy future, but some adjustments might have to be made.

Through a combination of the foods we choose to eat and our daily actions, we either create conditions in our bodies that support disease or an environment that support health. The universe is in a constant state of motion. You are either moving toward health or toward disease. You are either growing stronger or weaker. Think about your life and be totally honest... In which direction are you moving?

If you aren't happy with the answer, it is time to start making some changes.

Research is proving diet to be increasingly important in preparing our bodies to stay healthy and strong in the face of modern challenges. Eating a nutrient-dense diet can help the body rebuild and repair. This helps to keep our immune system functioning property. A strong immune system can help us to resist stress and provide protection from environmental factors that might otherwise cause disease (Greger, 2018). Please, do not take my word for it. Research an optimal nutrition program to ensure you are preparing your body and mind to be strong for our profession. While doing your research, remember that comprehensive health is about more than muscle mass - immune function, resiliency, and endurance also play very important roles.

    The standard American diet is one of the factors compromising our health. After spending years exploring the recommendations of the "health experts", I no longer believe these people have the best interest of any of us at heart. Equally concerning is the lack of education in nutrition-science that is required for medical doctors (Greger, 2018). *Heart.org* reports the average amount of training a doctor receives in their 10-12 years of specialty education is 19 hours. This education is often provided in a silo, and not interrelated to general health maintenance or causation of disease. It is like they are participating in the training just so they can check the box. I believe all of us in law enforcement know a great deal about how effective that approach to training is.

    This is a ridiculously low amount of time to spend on an area that has such a direct impact on health and wellness. I personally have had far more hours of education in nutrition through the specialty courses I have taken over the years. I tell you this to offer you a warning... Beware, the person who you think might be an expert may not actually have a great deal of information on how diet and nutrition relate to overall health. I beg you to empower yourself and do the research in these important areas on your own.

Recent findings within the scientific community are suggestive that each individual can actually make themselves "heart-attack proof" with effort (Greger, 2018). The science suggests this can be accomplished by having a total cholesterol level of under 140. The 140 number needs to be both the "good" cholesterol or high-density lipoprotein (HLD) and the "bad" cholesterol, or low-density lipoprotein (LDL) levels combined. Once my husband (also a police officer) and I learned it was possible to protect ourselves from one of the number one killers of law enforcement professionals, we decided to take action. One year later, we both had combined cholesterol levels well under 140. How did we do it? It was actually easier than you might think.

After doing research on how to most effectively lower cholesterol, we decided to switch to a plant-based diet. I know this is not an option that appeals to everybody, but I strongly suggest everyone at least commit to learning more about plant-based eating and the benefits it can bring before making a decision.

A great way to introduce yourself to the potential benefits of plant-based eating is the Netflix documentary *The Game Changers* (2018). While no one place has information I recommend any of us just blindly accept, this documentary is based in science and explores the myriad of benefits associated with plant-based eating, not just the potential for lower cholesterol levels. With the switch to plant-based eating my hubby and I saw our energy levels skyrocket and we have found a happier, healthier lifestyle. Visit www.mentaldominion.com for some of our favorite plant-based recipes.

My husband and I made the commitment to plant-based eating not only for ourselves, but also for our children. Too many cops die from heart-attacks and have their health compromised by other cardiac related issues. We decided it was our responsibility to take action to protect ourselves from *all* the threats associated with the work we love. While plant-based eating is not the only way to protect your health, it is one of the best. I encourage you to find the way that works best for you and make a commitment to living healthy.

Redefining Officer Safety

It is time to redefine both officer safety and officer wellness; and it is imperative we do so right now. With more officers losing their lives to suicide each year than all on-duty causes of death combined, it is clear mental health has not been a priority in our profession the way it needs to be. We must change this to protect ourselves and each other.

The COVID-19 pandemic crisis has shown us how underlying health issues can become a serious officer safety concern. While most of the country was under a stay-at-home order, police were out protecting and serving our communities as we always do. Policing during a pandemic brought a new level of attention to personal health and daily habits as we all struggled to remain safe during these unprecedented times.

If a police officer had an underlying health issue, the pandemic threat became even more serious. Those officers were still required to work in harm's way. Many officers lost their lives as a result of exposure to COVID-19 while working. In fact, as I am finishing this book COVID-19 has become the leading cause of line-of-duty deaths for police officers in 2020. This tragedy, more than any other I've seen in my more than two decades in law enforcement, shows the apex of where officer wellness and officer safety meet.

The stress of the job and the repeated exposure to traumatic events is causing a deadly mix for modern-day law enforcement officers. It is not only taking its toll on us physically, but also mentally. Officers who were once strong and ready for the challenges of this profession are finding themselves overwhelmed with frustration and aggravation caused by these and other factors present in our professional environment.

Civil unrest is another major issue. Police transitioned rapidly from having overwhelming public support to being criticized and condemned by a very vocal subset of society. With repeated exposure to this negativity and criticism of our profession, the spirit of our once strong and capable brothers and sisters is becoming compromised. Officers are being told to stand down and are working without the support of their employing organizations. This is causing a mass exit from our profession with many officers retiring earlier than they had ever planned. In extreme cases, this and other factors are causing police officers to give up the good fight and consider suicide as an option. Suicide in our profession is an epidemic. We cannot accept this any longer. Something must be done.

The elevated suicide rates seen in the law enforcement profession have been going on for too long. If we want this to change, we have to start doing something differently. I'm not talking about smashing the stigma here; I'm talking about something bigger than that. We need to learn to keep ourselves strong enough mentally to have the fortitude to make it through our careers. We have to do something to ensure the stress and repeated critical incident exposure that is part of the police experience will not continue to compromise our mental wellness. We need to start by understanding why this is happening at such a significant level in the law enforcement population.

Like the body, the mind can repair itself and gain strength as it heals and rebuilds from the challenges it faces. For the mind to do this, it needs rest and recovery time. While the brain is one of the body's organs, in this way it functions much like a muscle, having the ability to grow and develop when exposed to activity designed to build strength. Recovery time is an essential component of this process.

All police officers understand the importance of muscle recovery from a strength building perspective. Without sufficient time to rest, heal, and rebuild, a muscle that is constantly overworked will get weaker and not stronger. I know no police officer who would go to the gym and everyday strength train the same muscle group. We all know that would do more harm than good.

The mind operates under the same principles. Mental repair and rebuild is done during periods of sleep, mindfulness and meditation. Yet, police officers across the nation are ignoring this principle and making poor choices when it comes to brain rest and recovery. How many of us truly give our minds time to heal and repair before we start the heavy lifting again? Please do not get defensive and start blaming your department. This book is about ownership and learning a better way. We have more power over protecting our psyche than we might think.

We need to build both our physical and mental wellness to ensure we are prepared for the physical and psychological threats a career in law enforcement will surely bring. With intentional effort, we can make good choices and keep ourselves well. We need to get serious about protecting ourselves against the psychological threats of this profession to ensure we retire just as healthy as we were the day we started the job. This is something that can be done. This book will show you how.

Proactive Stress Management

The current generation of law enforcement officers understands to the depth of their being why proactive law enforcement efforts are more effective than reactive policing. Proactive policing means that officers are out in communities, working to identify issues and prevent problems before they begin. There is a focus on communication and collaboration when it comes to solving problems. In contrast, the reactive model has officers responding to problems after the fact. The damage has been done, and the officer is called in to try to pick up the pieces, solve the puzzle, and help the victims become whole again. When it comes to matters of police approach, the benefits of proactive initiatives are easy to see.

Similarly, officers can take that proactive mindset and apply it to matters of personal wellness. Each officer has the potential to take preventive action, to identify issues and to avoid risk factors in matters of health. Each of us can build collaborative relationships both within and outside of our profession that will help keep us mentally and physically strong. These relationships may be with care providers, health and wellness advocates and/or other members of a comprehensive support network. These connections will help us engage in intentional action that will reduce the occurrence of injury and illness. This will prepare us to be ready for both the physical and psychological threats of the police profession. Stress management is one area where proactive effort can have a huge positive impact.

Stress can have both favorable and unfavorable consequences when it comes to law enforcement. The stress of the job is often what makes our work exciting. The high level of training we receive in responding to high-risk situations allows us to become proficient in dealing with these volatile circumstances. Many professionals claim they thrive in the high-stress environment so commonly encountered by emergency service workers. The call to face danger or respond to an emergency puts them in the "zone." This is the place where preparedness is called into action and we are ready to respond with competency and confidence.

The feeling that you are in the "zone" is an example of performance that comes with a high level of training combined with the mastery of response. Any trainer will tell you this comes, in large part, from repetition of a task. Police officers know critical incidents create stress, but with sufficient training, the stress of the situation is often channeled as energy used to produce a skilled response. This is not unlike how a professional athlete performs on the field.

While the public often believes that the stress from critical incidents is where the disruptive stress of police work comes from, these occurrences are not typically the stressors that cause our police the most trouble. We train for critical incidents, and we know exactly how to respond when they present. When terrible things happen, we rise to the level of our training and perform at our professional best.

Where true police stress comes from is a very different place. To proactively manage our stress, the area we need to focus on are the daily chronic stressors present in our profession. These are the far more subtle yet constant stressors our modern-day police encounter. The smaller, everyday stressors we cannot seem to find a break from. These are the stressors that are destroying our resiliency and compromising our mental wellness.

When a major event occurs, as officers, we rise to the occasion. We take appropriate action and help resolve the situation. We are ready for this. We prepare for this stress; we train for critical incidents we hope we never see. If these unfortunate situations present, we are prepared to take necessary action to neutralize the threat and keep the public safe. If a terrible event does occur, we come together to care for one another. Because we are well prepared for these types of challenges, we often process the experiences in a different way. When the situation is over, we debrief, learn from the less than perfect parts, and move into the future better prepared for the next critical incident that will come our way.

It is the things we don't prepare for that are posing the real psychological threat. The day-to-day operational stressors are often the real concern of the police profession. The small things that police professionals see that slowly grind away at our coping skills. I am speaking of the things we almost never train for: the constant exposure to the negative, the impact of shift work and associated lack of sleep, and other areas that have been historically overlooked. These are the stressors that contribute to the negative psychological impact of the police profession. Just like an overworked muscle, when the brain continues to be exposed to these stressors day in and day out, they eventually compromise healthy functioning. This can result in an officer to experience reduced psychological resiliency and an inability to effectively manage stress.

For proof, just look at the Police Stress Study including a researcher who was a former police officer John Volanti. This study shows the daily stressors police are facing are causing negative physical and psychological health effects for the men and women in uniform (Gu, et al.,2012). While this may seem like a terrible finding, it is actually the key to making our profession healthier. Knowledge is power. With the knowledge that these health disparities have an occupational link, we can explore the potential underlying causes of this phenomenon and take action.

Sources of stress are not limited to the professional arena. Stress can come from many areas -- relationships, finances, parenting, educational endeavors, even leisure activities. The great thing about stress is, no matter where it comes from, a few simple techniques adopted as daily habits can help you manage it in a healthy and effective way.

We need to do more to protect ourselves. It's time for an officer wellness revolution.

Visit www.mentaldominion.com for a free workbook to accompany this book

Chapter 2: Action Steps for Positive Change

"If you feel "burnout" setting in, if you feel demoralized and exhausted, it is best, for the sake of everyone, to withdraw and restore yourself." -*Dalai Lama*

- Understand what you can do today to start to see positive changes in psychological resiliency
- Explain the importance of self-care from a mental wellness perspective
- Explore the research on meditation and mindfulness as it relates to law enforcement operations

Keep it Simple

The most effective stress management techniques are often the simplest. This means there are quick and easy interventions we can use to help us manage our stress. The trick to being successful with these interventions is to ensure we are practicing them as a regular part of our self-care routine. We must take intentional action.

As police, we know we cannot wait until we are challenged with a physical threat to develop our tactical skills. No one is waiting until they are faced with a deadly force situation to perfect their firearms proficiency or learn the rules of use of force. We understand the importance of preparedness when it comes to the physical threats of the profession. We need to prepare for psychological threats we continuously see in the same way.

Take Sleep Seriously

One of the best preventative stress management strategies a police officer can use is to get enough sleep. This means gone are the days of bidding midnights so you can do everything and be everywhere and then come to work in your spare time. Responsible habits include adhering to a set sleep and wake time as well as engaging in a healthy bedtime routine. Reading, taking a hot shower or bath, and meditating are all great ways to begin to relax the mind and transition to bedtime. Sometimes this is easier said than done.

While getting more sleep may seem like a cost effective and relatively simple solution, anyone who has worked shift work knows getting more sleep is not always easy to achieve. Interruptions seem to come from every angle. Overtime, social situations, and family obligations seem to constantly create a challenge. Sleep becomes something we fit in when we can find the time.

Planning to overcome these interruptions is one of the best ways we can increase our likelihood for success. The bedtime function available on many phones will send reminders/alerts for regular sleep and wake times. Even if we can't adhere to these set sleep times every single day, just having the reminder that we should be in bed is a great way to start creating healthier habits.

Keeping the television out of the bedroom and limiting screen time for approximately two hours before bed are other ways to help us wind down. Room darkening curtains and white noise machines can ensure external factors play a limited role in sleep disruption. Alcohol use, even in the mildest form is incredibly compromising to our ability to get healthy sleep. Alcohol disrupts not only the biochemistry of the brain, but also impacts the functioning of several other organs in the body inhibiting our ability to get deep, restorative sleep. Over the long term this can create chronic sleep disturbances and lead to even more health concerns. While these are some things we can control, often there are other factors also compromising our ability to sleep.

In some assignments, being on-call or other responsibilities may require the phone to be on the nightstand. If this is the case, use the settings to restrict calls from anyone except work. These intentional efforts can help us protect our sleep and ensure we are giving our brains the recovery time every healthy brain needs to maintain resiliency.

The importance of police getting serious about their sleep cannot be overstated. Schedule your sleep the same way you would a doctor appointment or some other important recurring event. Yes, exceptions can be made when special situations arise, but best practice is to establish a regular daily routine. If you are amongst the many who feel like there are not enough hours in the day, getting more sleep may seem impossible.

If this is your situation, I am telling you, I have been in your shoes. I understand your perspective, but please consider changing your relationship with sleep. When I changed my relationship with sleep using the strategies presented above, everything changed. I am willing to bet some of the reason you feel the way you do is because you are often tired. When people are tired things take longer. This causes the misperception that they don't have enough time to get everything done. This is caused by feeling mentally and physically exhausted when they don't need to be. More sleep makes this better. Let me provide this example to prove my point.

Running a mile itself is by no means an exhausting task. Even if we are not at an optimum fitness level, it is highly unlikely it would take any one of us more than fifteen minutes. If we had an adequate night's sleep, running a mile might be the warmup we do before we start our real workout. The part we do to warm our muscles up and get our heart pumping before we get into high-intensity interval training or our chosen workout for the day, certainly not the entirety of our effort.

Conversely, if we have not gotten a good night's sleep, running a mile might seem overwhelming. Something we could not possibly find the energy for. Just the thought of it might be exhausting. Now apply this consideration to all the things we do daily. The concept is universal.

When we get enough sleep, things are easier. They happen without effort. We are able to flow from one task to another with enthusiasm rather than having to drag ourselves from one thing to the next. I promise; with more sleep comes more energy. With more energy we can get more things done in less time. Please try it. It worked for me and it will work for you. I have more energy and motivation now than I had in my 20's and it is all because I get more sleep. It takes intentional action to create meaningful change. The choice to take action is up to you!

Let me be blunt. Lack of sleep is making us sick. Potentially more concerning than that, it is compromising our professional decision-making ability and negatively impacting our impulse control. This is a huge problem and one we need to start owning. One of the most important things we can do to ensure mental and physical health is get an adequate amount of sleep.

Overcoming Psychological Fatigue

The constant exposure to media sources is causing a mental ADHD throughout our society (Acher, 2010). This is not only making it difficult to sleep, it is also compromising our mental health in other ways. It is lessening our ability to focus and think deeply. It is compromising our ability to process complex situations in a responsible way. It throws us into a psychological state of reactivity taking away our ability to proactively problem solve and assess situations. For the modern-day police professional, this can have a detrimental effect.

From a mental health perspective, the media we consume is like the food we eat - it is either good for us or it is junk. It is almost impossible to be engaged in the world of social media and not have increased negative messaging exposure. The provocative headlines and partial stories we constantly consume cause our minds to run wild. This media exposure is like sugary snacks for the mind. There is nothing good that can possibly come from ingesting all that crap.

Subconsciously we are spending vast amounts of psychological energy trying to piece together the rest of the story. This is not a police-specific challenge, everyone does it, but it impacts us in a different way. This is because the ability to accurately assess situations is imperative for police. For law enforcement, understating the dynamic present in complicated situations is essential to our survival. This causes these headlines to consume our thought process and distract us at a different level.

Having our minds constantly bombarded with information is causing a state of psychological exhaustion for police professionals across the planet. To overcome this, we need to actively incorporate downtime into our daily routine. I am not talking about sleep. I am talking about peace and quiet.

If you ever find yourself in bed, completely exhausted but unable to turn off your mind and get to sleep, you are probably victim of this mental ADHD. Psychological exhaustion and physical exhaustion present the same in the human body. This means if you have a stressful day, you will feel physically tired when you are not. Just think of the last time you came home from work completely wiped out. It was likely not because you had been in a ten-mile foot pursuit, but because of all the stress you had to deal with as part of your workday. It does not matter if the stress came from your agency or from the street. By the time you finished your shift, you probably did not have the energy to take on much more. This is an example of psychological exhaustion.

It is here that police usually do the exact opposite of what we should be doing. If we feel depleted upon returning home from work, we need to shake it off and get moving instead of finding a comfy place on the couch and plugging into the TV. We all know exercise increases our energy levels. So instead of sitting around doing nothing, next time we feel exhausted at the end of a stressful day, we need to consider hitting the gym.

If we cannot manage the energy to get ourselves to the local fitness center, we need to go outside and take a walk or try a quick at home workout. Something like circuit training or a few sets of burpees will get our blood flowing and release the feel-good hormones that will bring our energy back. Exercise helps get rid of the excess cortisol levels from a stressful day and brings serotonin and dopamine back into our systems. We need these feel going hormones to reset the biochemical balance of our brains and help us feel normal again.

On the days we can't find the energy for any of those options, we can hop in the shower and let the water wash over us. Try making the water a little cooler than comfortable to really wake the body and clear the mind. It is only a matter of time before the stress of our day begins to wash away with the water and we begin to feel renewed.

Our Most Powerful Tool

Our mind is arguably the most powerful tool we have. Meditation is one of the activities intentionally designed to quiet the mind. Meditation can also work wonders to help ensure the brain is getting the rest it needs to restore itself and continue to function at its best. One of the best things about meditation is that it does not take a great deal of physical effort. So, if we truly feel too exhausted to do anything, meditation is an option to help reset the biochemical balance of the brain without moving a muscle.

That being said, meditation is not as easy as it may sound. It is worth putting effort into learning this skill. A Harvard research shows just a few minutes of meditation a day can increase the density of the grey matter of the brain (Schulte, 2015). This means meditation is to the brain as curls are to the biceps! A short session of meditation has been shown to have restorative effects on the brain and positive impact on quality of sleep (Rusch et. al, 2019). Meditation is something every police professional who is serious about taking care of their health should understand and explore.

As stated, meditation does take some time to learn, but there are few other skills that have such impressive beneficial psychological health results. Once mastered, meditation takes moments, costs nothing and can fast track the rest and recovery the police brain so desperately needs. This is an especially attractive option for those of us who find it a challenge to find the space in our lives to regularly get the recommended amount of sleep. Meditation can make the brain stronger, and stronger brains are more resilient to stress.

Meditation and mindfulness training have similar benefits to exercise interventions such as yoga, martial arts or distance running. All these activities can help you free yourself from distraction and be present in the moment. Local meditation centers and online videos are often available and provide instruction free of charge. If we find ourselves struggling to quiet that inner voice when trying to meditate, guided meditation is a great option. This approach has a calming voice talking us through the process and helps us focus our attention and minimize distractions. Guided meditation is a great tool but might not always be accessible when you need it. For a meditation option that is with you 24/7, breath meditation may be our best option.

Breath meditation ties the process of relaxing the brain to the body's natural breath cycle. As we are doing this, the mind will naturally start to wander. The power of this experience largely involves bringing our focus back to the breath and calming the mind. In doing this repeatedly, we show the mind that we are in control of our thought process. If the mind starts to wander while we are trying to focus on our breath, we simply release the distracting thought and bring our attention back to the breath. In doing this it is important to note we should not be trying to control your breath as we do in tactical breathing. Here we just notice the breath and focus the mind.

In breath mediation we bring our attention to how our body feels as we inhale and exhale. We feel the cool air enter our nostrils and the warm air escape our lips. This will help us eliminate any distracting thoughts and focus on the moment. It is amazing the calming impact a few mindful breaths can have on an overactive mind. Another approach to breath meditation involves using a mantra or calming word or phrase to have the same effect. This uses an intentional thought paired with the breath cycle to help bring focus and achieve a sense of calm.

Cultivating Mindfulness

Through meditation, we can create a state of focus commonly referred to as mindfulness. I want to make one thing very clear – mindfulness is not a distracted state. Common misconceptions believe meditation or mindfulness would put an officer into dreamlike state or a sleep-like trance. This is simply not the case.

Mindfulness is a state of a high level of presence and alertness without the distraction of the mind trying to multitask. It is pure focus. Quite simply, it is intentionally only thinking about one thing at a time. I know from experience there are non-busy moments in most shifts when we can afford to take a few moments and just be present. Of course, we must be selective about choosing those moments if we are going to use this technique while on duty. When police practice meditation and mindfulness we increase our brains ability to achieve a state of focus. Focus is an incredibly important skill for police to develop. Focus is what helps up perform our professional best when handling critical incidents or engaging in other high-risk activity such as emergency vehicle operations.

Most police encounter moments of mindfulness during their career without even realizing it. Mindfulness is what we are experiencing during those critical moments we spoke of earlier when our training kicks in and we are in "the zone". The practice of mindfulness will enhance the level of attention we can bring to all matters. With mindfulness training, we will start to notice the sights and sounds around us with a deeper level of attention. Overlooked details will begin to present themselves. Mindfulness is a powerful and effective skill for police to develop. We need to learn to harness mindfulness not only when we are responding to critical incidents, but on demand when we need to clear our minds from the unhealthy distractions of our everyday world.

Engaging with nature is another way to practice mindfulness and unplug from the information ambush we experience daily. Mindfulness is often a part of gardening, bird watching, or taking a hike. These activities can provide very similar benefits to meditation. In addition to that, nature provided fresh air and sunshine. Time spent in nature has positive health benefits for both the body and the mind. Getting outside is a great way to exercise mindfulness by paying attention to what is happening in the world around us.

Anything causing us to concentrate deeply for a prolonged period will bring about positive results. Meditation, mindfulness and connecting with nature are just a few ways to bring about these powerful benefits of a clear and present mind. By learning skills such as meditation and mindfulness, we can help ensure we have the psychological resilience needed to continue to thrive in this profession. With practice, these healthy habits will not only help us work happy, but we will see improvements in our quality of life outside of work.

Step Outside the Uniform

When we started this profession, all of us used to have activities we liked to do outside of work. Working out, home improvement projects, and outdoor activities usually topped the list. A brain that has been chronically exposed to stress can start to lose the ability to enjoy the simpler things in life. If we are not careful, as the stress of the profession begins to get to us, we start to become consumed with a sense of psychological exhaustion. When this occurs, we will no longer have the energy for our favorite hobbies. Even more upsetting, we will start to lose our ability to enjoy anything at all.

Think of the last time you went out and did something just for the enjoyment of it. Not because you promised someone, not because you felt obligated - something you did just for you. If you cannot remember easily, it has probably been too long. And for the record, going to the bar and getting drunk does not count.

The more our personal and professional identities merge, the less we remember who we are without the job. Many law enforcement professionals give their heart and soul to this profession. While this can make us very effective police officers, it can bring compromise to our sense of self. It is important to stay engaged in a variety of activities and keep a group of friends who have interests outside of law enforcement. Each of us needs to remember there is a person inside our uniform. That person deserves to have a life outside of work. That person deserves to have frequent moments of joy and relaxation.

Building activities into our schedule intended to increase enjoyment are essential components of mental health. Once again, intentional action and effort is required to make this happen. We need to start exploring activities we have always been curious about and learn something new. The brain builds strength each time it develops new knowledge.

We need to develop the habit of scheduling these activities into our days as frequently as possible. In order to accomplish this, we are going to have to go out of our way to find the time to invest in this component of self-care. Doing this will help us ensure we find balance between who we are as people and who we are as professionals. These personal interests will enhance our quality of experience in both areas. Having a variety of interests outside work makes us more diverse law enforcement officers. Taking time to do things we enjoy will not detract from our commitment to our profession, it will engage us at a higher level.

Invest Wisely

What are your priorities? Please take a moment and make a list.

Now that you have that list, I want you to think about how you spend your time. Are you spending your time on the things that are most important to you? Do your priorities even show up as significant time investments when you look at how the hours of your day are spent? Or, on most days, are you spending all your time on work and other tasks?

It is crucial that we all invest our time on what is most important in our lives. Please do not miss this point. This is one of the most important details in ensuring you maintain healthy relationships with the people we love. Time, not money, is the currency of love. The people in our world who love us do not care how much money we make. They don't care how fancy the vacations we take them on are or how many gifts we buy for them... they just want to spend time with us. They want to get to know us. They want to connect. They want to talk to us and listen to us and laugh with us. We need to adjust our habits now to invest time in those relationships before it is too late.

We all must work. We know how demanding the police profession can be. We understand how tempting it can be to take a much-needed vacation and indulge a little. There is a strong pull for most of us to make our homes into places we can truly enjoy when we are off duty. We are gone so much we want to make sure our family has all they need, so we go out and buy those unnecessary little extras attempting to keep everyone happy. But all those luxuries cost money. We need to take care to ensure in attempting to provide all these things, we do not overextend ourselves financially. Overspending can be a very slippery slope that can compromise our ability to invest your time in our priorities.

One or two indulgent purchases are probably not going to cause too significant of an impact. The problem is many of us can get caught up in a cycle where they are overspending in an effort to try and build much-needed relaxation and enjoyment into their world. Often this results in the police officer needing to compensate by working more to ensure financial stability. This additional workload leaves less time for the very relaxation we are trying to achieve.

If this has become your reality, please pause for a moment, and consider what I said earlier- time is the currency of love. It is far more important that you spend time with the important people in your world than it is that you take them on lavish vacations. I promise. They just want to see you. Far too many police professionals have lost marriages and relationships over poor time investment. If any one of your family members have ever stated that it seems that you love the job more than you love your family, you need to stop and take notice. This might be happening to you.

I lost a marriage and severely damaged a relationship with my stepdaughter over this very thing. I did not do it on purpose- I was trying my hardest to save for the future and provide the lifestyle I thought they wanted. As I continued to go to work to try and create what I thought was the perfect life, these important relationships were slowly crumbling. All they wanted was for me to spend more time at home. By the time I realized it, it was too late.

The proceeding sections have presented just a few of the many tactics police can apply to ensure we are taking a proactive approach to managing stress. As mentioned before, it is best if we adopt these habits early on in our careers and practice them daily. It is never too late to start to make positive changes. Do not wait until the challenge of stress causes problems before you start to manage it. To do so would be a reactive approach that will not produce optimal results. Train on healthy stress management habits each day to ensure those skills are solid for the moment that stress challenge presents. All of us need to commit to intentional time investments to ensure we are protecting our psychological health. This is the best way to ensure we are prepared to protect ourselves against the psychological threats of the profession.

Learning about stress management is vital because law enforcement is one of the most stressful professions there is. This is true in times of peace, and especially true in times of civil unrest. If we are going to commit ourselves to serving society in a high-stress profession, we need to be serious about committing ourselves to learning how to handle that stress. We need to understand how serious the threat of unmanaged stress is for police.

Stress as a Safety Threat

Stress is not traditionally something we can see or touch. This intangibility at times makes it seem like less of a threat to our safety than something more concrete like a man with a gun. It is my hope by the end of this book that the psychological threats of this profession, such as stress, will be viewed as just as legitimate of a threat as a physical assailant. To do that, I need to dive a little deeper into the research on stress.

Stress is a universal concept. While police have more stress, and one could even argue different stress than the general population, stress is stress. Police training teaches many officers to handle stressors that could be overwhelming to the untrained, unexposed public. As part of this job, we see the worst of the worst. We become desensitized and learn to accept violence and crime as part of an average workday. Research suggests it is the exposure itself that is having a compromising effect on the men and women serving our profession.

Due to the advent of trauma-informed policing, many law enforcement professionals now are familiar with ACES (Adverse Childhood Experience Score) and how they can negatively impact an individual's functioning later in life. In many academic studies the relationship between disruptive experiences in childhood and the likelihood for chronic health problems as adults were found to be closely related.

There are two significant research findings that have the potential to tell us how traumatic event exposure relate to mental health. The first is that there is a direct link between childhood trauma exposure and the adult onset of chronic disease (including mental illness). The second finding that I believe is relevant for understanding wellness is the more adverse exposure a child has (the higher the number of ACES), the greater the risk of mental and physical illness later in life (Stevens, 2012). I doubt any police officer is surprised by these findings. The question we need to be asking is how does this relate to police wellness?

While this study was conducted on children; research is starting to uncover how repeated, long-term critical incident exposure might be having a similar effect on the adult brain. The occurrence of Post-Traumatic Stress may be the most significant example of this correlation. This will be discussed in further detail shortly. To help explain why I believe this is something we need to know about, I would like to present a chart created from the data presented in the article.

```
                    Early Death
              Disease,
           Disability and
          Social Problems
       Adoption of Health-risk
              Behaviors
      Social, Emotional and Cognitive
                Impairment
         Disrupted Neurodevelopment
         Adverse Childhood Experiences
```

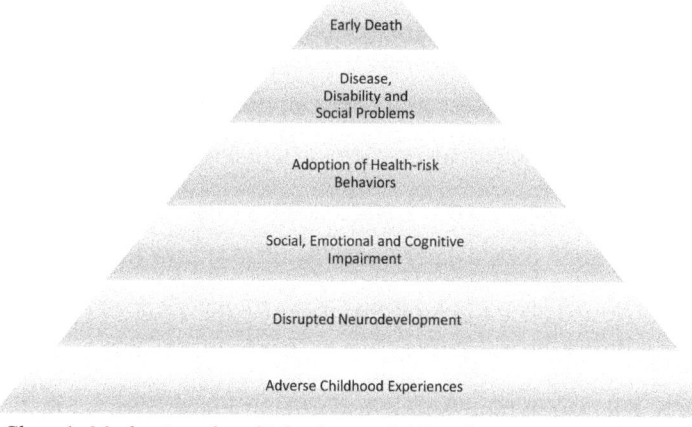

Chart 1- Mechanisms by which adverse childhood experiences influence health and well-being of an individual throughout their lifetime

This chart clearly demonstrates how ACES disrupts the neurodevelopment of a child, causing them to be at greater risk for the development of chronic disease. This causes one to question if critical incident exposure in adulthood could potentially have a similar impact.

After spending more than ten years researching the impact of stress on the health of police professionals, I believe this is what is happening to police. The negative impact of adverse/traumatic experiences has the ability to cause changes to the brain at any age. This is causing social, emotional and cognitive impairment for police officers. This impairment is creating many challenges that are directly related to our ability to stay psychologically healthy over the course of our careers.

We all know adults exposed to critical incidents can develop post-traumatic stress (PTS). This PTS can be so disruptive it can cause a change in how the affected person processes the world. Research is just starting to embark on how *chronic* traumatic incident exposure can potentially have the same impact. This is all emerging psychological science that holds great hope for a deeper understanding of how the critical incidents we see as part of our professional experience might be causing real issues for police professionals. Not only in the form of PTS, but also in more subtle ways in our home environments.

Research suggests it is possible repeated exposure to traumatic events in adulthood increase the likelihood for mental and physical illness later in life the same way the higher the number of ACES result in the greater risk for children. If this is in fact true, this could be part of the reason police professionals see such high rates of depression, addiction and divorce. It could also be the reason for law enforcements elevated rates of heart disease, diabetes and cancer. What is happening on the job could literally be making us physically and mentally unwell. The job might actually be killing us.

The following chart demonstrates what this could look like for police professionals who started this occupation both mentally and physically healthy but were then exposed to repeated traumatic incidents along the way.

- Early Death
- Disease, Disability and Social Problems
- Adoption of Helth-risk Behaviors
- Social, Emotional and Cognitive Impairment
- Changed Neuroprocessing due to Repeated Traumatic Event Exposure
- Mentally and Physically Strong Officer

Chart 2- Mechanisms by which repeated traumatic event exposure influence health and well-being of an officer throughout their career and beyond

The ACES study proves trauma exposure at certain stages of development can increase an individual's likelihood for both mental and physical disease. Research suggests this is not only true for children, but also adults. When considering police traumatic incident exposure, we need to look at the repeated incidents of death and destruction seen by police. Continuous exposure to human violence and vicious criminal intent are other areas that could be causing psychological trauma. Police are also repeatedly exposed to tragic accidents and people taking their own lives. How could anyone think this level of traumatic incident exposure seen repeatedly over a 20 to 30-year career is not going to have some type of psychological impact?

While these traumatic experiences are different from what the ACES questionnaire measures, they are traumatic experiences, nonetheless. Common sense dictates they must have an impact on how the officer processes the world. This is likely causing similar disrupted neurodevelopment seen in children exposed to trauma as measured by the ACES assessment.

Take a moment and ask yourself if this job has changed you. If you want an accurate assessment you should probably ask someone who knew you before you got on the job. If you can see differences in your personality, it is likely this has been caused by a change in the way your brain interprets the world (a change in nueroprocessing). I am suggesting this is associated with constantly seeing the darkest side of humanity.

Police are called to respond to the mad, bad and sad in our society. We are tasked with looking deeply into criminal behavior and exploring underlying motives. Soon we start to notice these signs all around us. Indicators of criminal intent are apparent everywhere. Our brain begins to look for the negative because that's our job! The effect this is having can no longer be ignored. Protective measures must be taken.

These changes are having a negative impact on our happiness and our health. All we have to do is look at the typical officer's longevity rates after retirement to know something is compromising our ability to remain healthy in this profession. The rate of law enforcement suicide, divorce, and addiction shows us there is also a negative impact on our psychological well-being. Whether we want to admit it or not, this is suggestive of a compromise of social, emotional, and cognitive impairment as the previous chart indicates. This is concerning because it is compromising not only our mental and physical health, but also our ability to maintain healthy relationships.

The fact that police have a higher rate of addiction, depression and divorce is not some type of bizarre coincidence. That we, occupationally, have a higher likelihood to develop disease is also not coincidental. We have long known something happening on the job is making it difficult for us to stay healthy. The repeated traumatic event exposure is likely to be directly responsible.

A change in neuroprocessing causes us to develop a negative world view. Instead of being hopeful and optimistic, we learn to be critical and suspicious. We no longer believe all people are good and instead believe there is a nefarious undertone present in the world. We have seen so much selfish criminal behavior we believe any altruistic effort made by members of society is fueled by some sort of personal gain we haven't yet figured out. We find things irritating instead of amusing, suspicious instead of innocent. A darkness has settled in and it has changed the way we perceive everything. All this is occurring on the inside, often undetected, until the impact begins to affect our lives.

How does this manifest in our lives? Our relationships are strained. We start pushing people we love away because our jaded view of the world has caused us to doubt their good intentions. We have seen pillars of society do the most horrible things imaginable and we convince ourselves the fewer close friends we have the more protected we are from something terrible happening in our inner circle. We are self-medicating to mute the memories of the tragic realities we have seen. We complain about absolutely everything. We learn to focus on the negative in the world and lose our ability to see the positive things that happen around us each and every day. These factors are priming us for dysfunction, chronic disease, and early death. We must do something to intervene and reclaim our mental and physical health.

Chapter 3: A Critical Look at Police Suicide

"It is no measure of health to be well adjusted to a profoundly sick society." — *J. Krishnamurti*

- Understand why law enforcement suicide is different from suicide amongst members of the general public
- Explore what factors in our profession might be contributing to our high suicide rates
- Understand the research into police suicide and how we can use this knowledge to give us the power to stop this phenomenon now

Stop Accepting the Unacceptable

Suicide is a problem our profession must address aggressively and immediately. It is not the only concerning issue we see in law enforcement. Pessimism, divorce, anger, and an unhealthy relationship with alcohol, are other areas resulting in a compromised quality of life. These factors are prevalent at such a significant level that they have caused many police officers to believe it is nearly impossible to stay healthy in such an unhealthy profession.

Police suicide has haunted the law enforcement profession for decades. Recent efforts to shed light on this dark secret have increased awareness and somewhat reduced the stigma of seeking mental health services, but still the problem persists. In working to better comprehend why this is happening, it is not only important that we understand suicidality in general but also police suicidality specifically. This chapter will explore both the realities and causes of police suicide. It will also offer action steps on how you can protect yourself from suicide becoming a threat to your personal safety.

As a generational law enforcement officer who not only saw my father changed by the profession, but also struggled personally to remain healthy throughout my career, the concept of officer "wellness" has become a personal passion. The journey to discovering building blocks of wellness has been fascinating, but terrible at the same time. In researching this topic, I found it impossible to explore officer wellness in a meaningful way without going into the depths of darkness to better understand officer suicide.

Why is this Happening?

I have spent more than ten years researching this topic to try to understand what is happening to law enforcement professionals that is causing our high rates of suicide. More than simply wanting to identify a cause, I wanted to understand why it was occurring and if anything could be done to stop it. I am not alone in my efforts; I have met remarkable people in my journey who are doing incredible work around this important issue. Together, we are finally starting to make some progress.

It is easy to see that many of the situations handled by a police officer during his or her career might be deeply disturbing. The horrific events we see as part of our normal work experience could be contributing factors to the elevated suicide rates seen in the profession. It is possible some members of our profession are haunted by memories they cannot escape. The research suggests it is more than the trauma exposure we discussed in the last chapter that contributes to law enforcement suicidality. In this chapter we will identify the risk factors police are exposed to in attempt to better prepare officers to overcome the psychological threats they are facing each and every day they put on the uniform.

We have discussed traumatic event exposure and the negative impact these experiences may be having on our mental and physical health. Now that this is identified, we need to better understand the details of how repeated traumatic event exposure might play into our suicide epidemic. We also need to understand if this is even part of the suicide conversation, or if there are larger and more complex factors that need to be considered.

We cannot just accept that the stress of this profession is unmanageable and creating an early death sentence, either from compromised health or from our own hand. There is a way to stay physically and psychologically strong despite all we are exposed to. To identify these strategies and ensure they become part of our law enforcement culture, it will take intentional effort and action. My belief is the more we understand police suicide, the better prepared we will be to stop it.

A Critical Look

It is impossible to conduct an evaluation of every law enforcement suicide. People are inherently different. Each individual and all the complicated circumstances involved in their unique situation will present details unlike any other. There are many complicating factors contributing to the lack of understanding of this phenomenon.

One of the most obvious difficulties with understanding why a person committed suicide is the fact that the person is gone. Because of this we cannot ask the person what led up to the suicide decision. We have no way to know what their thought process was. We are unable to ask if there was one thing that happened that pushed them past the point of no-return. We usually do not even investigate these situations the way we would investigate another type of death. There is so much devastation and pain left behind, we do not want to ask any questions that might, somehow, make matters worse.

The person is gone and that cannot be undone. Piecing things together somehow seems insensitive to the family. Even if the officer left a note, it is unlikely that the note contains all the answers for those who remain behind. We know there is more to the story, but we are often unable to uncover the details that led to that tragic moment. We are heartbroken and defeated every time this occurs.

To try and understand the complexities of the human mind and this destructive course of decision making is an incredibly challenging task. Even if the individual were here to answer questions, it would still be difficult to understand emotional-based reasoning. Emotion and logic operate in different parts of the brain. This is the reason it is so difficult to rationalize with a hysterical person. When people are emotionally elevated, often their logical brain simply does not work.

Emotion is regulated in our low brain; that lizard brain that houses our instincts. Logic, on the other hand, is a function of our prefrontal cortex, our higher order human brain. Suicidality is often the result of an individual feeling a certain way (isolated, misunderstood, ashamed, depressed), and those emotion-based thoughts are often driving their actions in that critical moment. When the emotional brain is in control, often there is flawed logic associated with the decision-making process. This makes it difficult for the rest of us to understand the thought process leading to the suicide decision.

Research shows the desire to live and the desire to die can exist simultaneously in the brain (Joiner, 2005). This confuses not only the affected individual, but also makes it more difficult for anyone on the outside to understand their reasoning. The unique circumstances of an individual officer's life might be extraordinary and unlike any other officer. This individuality causes researchers to look for overarching themes to increase our understanding of suicide. This is done in the hope commonalities can be found within these themes to help us understand the phenomenon as it relates to the larger police population.

The themes can then potentially help us understand and address the unacceptable rate of suicide we have been seeing in our profession. In 2019, Blue H.E.L.P. reported 228 suicides. That same year, Officer Down Memorial Page reported 134 officers dying in the line-of-duty. That line-of-duty number includes gunfire, auto-related incidents, and more than a dozen other causes of line-of-duty death. Each year, our profession looks at these numbers, assesses potential threats to officer safety, and implements training in attempt to address the issue and keep our officers as safe as possible.

While the police profession continues to train for and discuss the elevated levels of violence in our society, the fact is more officers die by their own hand than do in all line-of-duty deaths combined. We need to start looking at our suicide rate, conducting the same type of assessment, and start educating and training our officers in a different way. How can one cause, suicide, be almost twice as lethal as all line of duty causes combined? Maybe more importantly, how has our profession allowed this to continue to happen? And now that we are finally talking about it, what can be done to stop it? This chapter will explore what research says about police suicide and offer some action steps you can implement today to protect yourself from this very real safety threat.

Resisting Help

Research has identified several factors as potentially having an impact on police suicide. One of these often-misunderstood concepts is something known as "perceived burdensomeness" (Hill & Pettit, 2014; Joiner, 2017). Simply stated, perceived burdensomeness suggests people don't want to be a drain on anyone else. Police can have a difficult time moving from their professional role as helper to the role of the one needing help in their personal life. This is important for both the police officer and the police officer's family to know. After spending years always being called on to help others, becoming the person asking for help can make an officer feel vulnerable. And the innate dangers of the job cause police to process the feeling of vulnerability as a threat to officer safety.

When a threat to officer safety occurs, police are trained to find a course of action that will eliminate that threat. The sense of vulnerability an officer experiences is the same whether the threat comes from a physical or psychological source. Often, when the threat is physical, officers can take cover, create distance, or take other action to ensure they are safe.

When the threat is psychological, our response is quite different. We do not train annually for the threats we don't see. Our default course of action seems to be denying a problem exists and pretending nothing is wrong. This is one of the dynamics that could be keeping police professionals from asking for intervention. It might not be a resistance to asking for help, so much as an attempt to suppress a feeling of vulnerability that makes us feel unsafe.

What complicates this matter ever further is the flawed logic that emotionally charged situations can produce. If a police officer believes he or she could become a burden, then he or she may intentionally seek out ways to ensure that does not happen. When complicated situations occur on the job, our supervisors encourage us to use our resources to find creative solutions. In matters of personal distress, often those resources are limited to our current knowledge base. They may even be influenced by the police professional's exposure to the outside world and the way they see others handling their problems. This can be deadly considering current trends.

Think about your career for a moment. How many suicides have you seen firsthand? How many are you aware of within your community? How many law enforcement brothers and sisters do you know of who have selected suicide as an option? If you are honest, the numbers are staggering.

As mentioned earlier, in 2019, U.S. law enforcement reported 228 suicides. In fact, if you add up the numbers, law enforcement has seen nearly 1,000 police suicides in the past five years. Our awareness of these tragedies contributes to our knowledge base. Police officers must take protective measures to ensure this does not become their internal definition of how police deal with personal problems. Unless we take a firm stand that suicide is not an acceptable option in each and every one of our agencies, these numbers will continue to cripple our profession. We cannot allow that to happen.

We must start training police on how to overcome the psychological threats of this profession with the same intensity as we train for the physical threats we encounter on the street. We must let our officers know there is a way to keep the brain resilient and strong. Pretending we are ok is not the answer. We must empower our officers to take personal responsibility for their mental wellness. Only then will we see officers understanding the importance of taking proactive action to ensure mental wellness.

Smashing the stigma and encouraging officers to ask for help will work for some officers but not all of them. We need to find a way to get in front of this. We need to find a way to keep our officers well instead of waiting until they are compromised and trying to undo damage that has already occurred. Proactive efforts designed to protect mental wellness need to become part of our new narrative.

Being Part of Something

Thwarted belonging is another concept that research suggests is relevant to understanding suicide. "Thwarted belongingness" is a sense of social disconnectedness from others (Joiner, 2005). Feeling a lack of connection to the people closest to you can leave a person feeling isolated and lonely. This becomes especially significant if a strong sense of belonging once existed or is desired. Law enforcement is a profession filled with teams that operate based on this sense of belonging. Whether it be a shift, a specialty unit, or a fraternal organization, as police officers, a large part of our identity is established based on the groups we belong to.

Once a person becomes a police officer, the professional life ties directly into their personal identity. This can cause police to feel like outcasts in society, especially during times of civil unrest. Police are different. We enforce the rules. We provide consequences for criminal behavior. This is often unpopular.

Police are held to a higher standard. We have a code of ethics we must follow. A bad decision resulting in a breach of moral character can cost us our jobs. We are never off duty. When police go to work, we put a gun on our hip and strap Kevlar to our chests. We know we might have to place ourselves in harm's way to protect the innocent. We know we might not go home. There are very few professions that require this type of self-sacrificing commitment.

The dangers in society are real and it is impossible for police to know when these dangers might present themselves. We need to be ready. This sense of readiness, the hypervigilance, the need to sit with your back to the wall and see the door in the restaurant, these are real factors and they make police different from other members of society. Our responsibility to protect others becomes part of our identity. This is the group police belong to. We are the brave… the prepared… the protectors.

The desire to belong is a basic human need. For police, this sense of belonging is also a part of the officer's professional identity. When the group membership ends or is denied, an officer can experience a sense of separation that makes him or her feel less than whole. When that happens, it is often accompanied by a deep sense of loss. This can present as an overwhelming feeling that something is wrong. During these challenging times, it can be difficult to remember the connections that make life meaningful.

The officer may begin to self-isolate, identifying other people and their decisions as the source of the emotional pain. Often this occurs on a subconscious level, but the resulting actions are the same. The isolation associated with thwarted belonging can contribute to thoughts of insignificance and increase suicidal ideology. This, combined with the way police perceive the world and their desensitization to death, create a deadly mix.

Thwarted belonging can happen when the disconnection occurs within the professional environment or in the officer's personal life. There are many real challenges that make it difficult for police to connect to those they love. This often starts with a well-intentioned desire to protect your loved ones from the terrible things you see at work. Imagine someone asking about your day at work after a shift where you handled a horrific crash. You don't want to discuss the details. Hell, you wish you could get it out of your head, you surely are not going to bring it home to your family. You feel exhausted (remember psychological exhaustion presents in the human body as fatigue). You do not feel like engaging in much conversation at dinner that night. You feel too tired to talk. Your spouse mentions you seem distracted. You are distracted. Situations like this are where disconnection slowly begins to creep in and compromise our personal relationships.

If this scenario, or something similar, plays out week after week, month after month, disconnection will eventually develop. This loss of connection in a meaningful relationship can lead to thwarted belonging. The good news is it is possible to apply intentional action to stop this from happening. Through intentional proactive intervention, we can do our part to keep ourselves connected.

Scheduling intentional date nights or mini getaways where there is no talking or thinking about work is a fun way to start. Having a friend or co-worker you can call and vent to when work is distracting you is another great option. Physical activity will always help improve your mood and bring focus. Meditation can help us bring intention to our thought process and help us contain unwelcome or distracting thoughts. On those super stressful days, try hitting the gym after shift for a quick workout, or taking a nice long walk after you get home to clear your mind. By doing these things before disconnection begins, we improve our chances of maintaining healthy relationships despite the stress of our chosen profession.

Negative Sentiment Override

At the start of a police career, young, optimistic candidates put their best effort forward to become police officers, to devote their lives to helping society. Officer applicants often go through an arduous testing process that involves cognitive, physical, and mental screening tests to ensure they are mentally and physically strong enough to meet the demands of a career in law enforcement. If the individuals pass all the testing, interviewing, and screening, they are hired. The training for a life as a public servant begins.

Any officer reading this book probably remembers these early days of their own law enforcement career. The excitement, the enthusiasm, and the willingness to help on any incident defines the first few years of almost every young police professional's life. It seems like a dream. Then something happens.

Every day, that officer is called to incidents involving the most negative components of human existence. They are called to help people who are hurt, victimized, or have seen various levels of tragedy. At some point, this daily exposure to the worst parts of the human experience does something to compromise the optimistic perspective of the young officer. This phenomenon has been referred to as disillusionment, becoming a realist, and other less appropriate things. Whatever you want to call it, as we discussed, the job changes us.

This change is what the chart in Chapter 2 was designed to explain. Just like a strong physical body can get hurt, so can even the strongest human mind. With enough exposure to compromising events, any human psyche will start to weaken. That is unless we learn how to protect ourselves. We must learn to build psychological resilience.

Imagine something basic like strength training. If a strong person picked up a 20-pound barbell and decided to do some curls, at first this would be done with ease. If this individual decided to complete repetitions to muscle failure, the weight (which seemed so manageable at first) would be near impossible to lift as the muscles of the arm reached a state of fatigue. The human psyche works the same way - it can only take so much.

Many years ago, when lateral transfers were not quite as popular as they are today, getting hired by another agency was a real area of concern. The biggest threat to an officer getting hired at the new agency was if he or she could pass the psychological test at the new department. Even though this was the same psychological test the officer had just passed a few years before, for some reasons, it seemed like many officers, once on the job, would "fail" the exam.

For years, people misunderstood why this was happening. Officers across the nation experienced the exact same phenomenon. The same story was told time and time again. First time around, the person passed the psychological test without a problem. The job offer came along and the new officer spent several years working on the street and learning the profession. The individual was becoming a fine young officer.

After some time on the job, the grass seems greener (for whatever reason) on another agency and the officer wants to explore working over there. When that time comes, the same officer would take the exact same psychological test. Only this time there was a real threat the officer might not pass. How was this possible? At the time, the best explanation seemed to be that psyche tests were "hit or miss" or dependent on your "mood" for the day.

This phenomenon was happening so consistently that someone decided to research why it was occurring. It appears that constant exposure to the negative elements of society combined with the level of assertiveness required to successfully handle emergency situations was subtly changing parts of the police professional's psychological profile. Universally, as officers spent time on the job, they were becoming more assertive, desensitized to violence, and less optimistic. This change was having an impact on the results of the psychological test. The concerning part is not only the change in profile, it is the change in personality that comes with elevations in those areas. These are the same neurological changes that might be compromising officer wellness.

Through the repeated exposure to emergency situations, officers working the street developed nerves of steel. Blood, dark places, spiders, and other things that may have been slightly bothersome before were now areas where officers were desensitized due to repeated exposure. The more time an officer spent on the job, the more pronounced the impact of this desensitization. This change was being picked up on in those psychological profiles and causing a non-normal or elevated profile on some areas of the psychological assessment.

A civilian with no exposure to dangerous or unsettling situations would report the scenarios presented on the psychological examination to be much more disturbing than a police officer would. This desensitization was further skewed by the other changed areas of the psychological profile of the officer. The assertiveness was creating what appeared to be an elevated level of aggression. The lack of trust created by continuous exposure to the criminal element was creating a profile presenting as low-level paranoia. Put this all together and the result of exposure to repeated critical incidents was creating a "police profile." This was causing applicants who had prior police experience to fail the psychological test.

Understandably, elevations in some areas of assessment were a direct result of skills developed intentionally during training. If the officer did not demonstrate an ability to be assertive in field training, they likely would not have remained employed. This new level of assertiveness was being picked up on by the test as another elevated area. While this was not happening to every officer, the more exposure to the dark side of society an officer had during his or her time on the job, the more likely this was to become a reality.

Research to the Rescue

Officers saw what was happening on the psychological tests but couldn't explain it. The psychological community realized this was happening but didn't fully understand why. It was only when a similar set of challenges began affecting our military professionals exposed to combat that people started to study and understand this phenomenon.

As a result of the identification of how the brain changes due to trauma or critical incident exposure, experts created a restructured form of one of the most commonly used psychological assessments which now includes a police candidate interpretative report (Corey& Ben-Porath, 2014). This allows for elevation considerations of both behavior and personality characteristics specific to people with prior police or military experience. Thankfully, this psychological test has taken the place of other versions of the assessment that resulted in people with police experience struggling to present profiles within normative ranges. The revised assessment is one of the reasons officers today can transfer agencies without unnecessary fear of failing the psychological evaluation.

The revised format of the inventory compensates for the areas of elevation that before were triggering as elevated areas of concern. These areas of elevation are now recognized as normal for people repeatedly exposed to trauma and critical incidents.

Our professionals are no longer failing psychological tests after spending time on the job. This is allowing them to test for other departments and change employers with success. While that's great news, it does not address how these elevated areas are affecting us in our personal relationships or as professionals who work with the public every single day.

There can be no doubt that police work changes the psyche of the law enforcement officer. Police see the world differently, and while this in and of itself is not bad, it presents a dynamic we need to recognize and respond to. The changes in elevation in those subsets of our psychological profile that occur due to critical incident exposure are bound to affect us in day-to-day matters. This will present as a challenge for officers both personally and professionally. Specifically of interest is how these changes might increase our propensity for risk of suicide. This will be discussed in great depth in the next chapter.

It is important we protect ourselves to the best of our ability from the negativity of the profession. This should start with using the proactive stress management techniques discussed in previous chapters. Intentionally scheduling activities we enjoy and spending time with loved ones can ensure we are regularly exercising our happy brain muscles, retaining their strength. Exposure to fresh air and sunshine, eating healthy foods, and expressions of gratitude are other proven ways to overcome negative sentiment override. When several of these proactive approaches are used in harmony, we can build psychological resiliency. This will result in us being better prepared for the psychological threats of our profession and put us on the road to sustained mental wellness.

Chapter 4: Reducing the Threat of Suicide

*"Everyone thinks of changing the world, but no one thinks of changing himself."- **Leo Tolstoy***

- Learn what the research suggests about why people attempt suicide in some situations but not others
- Explore the differences between situational stress and operational stress
- Understand practical steps police professionals can take to reduce the risk of suicide

Deadly Force and Self-Harm

As departments hire police officers, one of the first things they do is issue a duty weapon as one of the many necessary tools of the trade. The firearm is more than just another component of the police uniform. It clearly defines the highest level of trust society places on the police - the discretion to use deadly force. This tool shows the level of confidence and trust the general public has for police authority, and the power associated with this level of trust cannot be betrayed. It is part of the pride of the profession. Total strangers trust us to wield this power in a state of grace and humility as we walk among them.

At the academy, police officers receive training on the appropriate use of force in complex, dynamic, rapidly changing circumstances. Through this training, the highest calling is always the protection of life. Part of the training that police receive is an exposure to the reality that in a certain set of circumstances— to protect their own life or that of another—a police officer may have to use deadly force against someone. This is a necessary part of police training.

The problem is, when we introduce the police recruit to the concept that they may need to use that weapon to take a life, it is never explained to the officer that under no circumstances should that duty weapon be used for self-harm. It is no coincidence that many police officers preferred method of suicide is with their duty weapon. It is time to take a deeper look at some of the reasons for this unfathomable truth.

"Coupling" and Suicidal Intent

In Malcolm Gladwell's 2019 book *Talking to Strangers*, he discusses the concept of coupling as it relates to suicide in the civilian population of England. This is a provocative concept that posits the act of suicide being closely connected, or coupled, to the method of suicide. The research suggests that people become very emotionally attached to their preferred method, and if that chosen method is not available and easy to access in the vulnerable moment when suicidal thoughts happen, then people do not explore other methods of lethal self-harm. The suicide simply does not occur.

Gladwell describes a phenomenon from the 1950s and 1960s related to the increase in occurrences and consistency of method of death by suicide in England. In this era, the fuel for ovens in English homes was something Gladwell refers to as "town gas." Town gas was a fuel created by heating coal to high temperatures in airtight chambers, which was then delivered to individual homes to fuel their stoves and water heaters. The fuel was a very clean-burning mixture of a variety of gases including methane, hydrogen, nitrogen, and the deadly carbon monoxide. In 1962, almost half (44%) of the 5,588 suicides in England and Wales were completed with the use of town gas. Some people placed their heads in their ovens, while others piped the toxic gas into their lungs in other ways. In the late 1960s, England started transitioning homes to the use of natural gas, which was much safer. The question Gladwell poses is what happened to the suicide rate in these counties when house gas was no longer available as a method of suicide.

It would seem likely that the suicide rate would be relatively consistent. One would think taking the town gas out of the homes would have little to no impact on those who were truly suicidal. If the quick and easy way—in this situation, the gas supply to the oven—was not available, then people would just find another method. In our limited understanding, we have a tendency to believe if one method is removed, that people who want to commit suicide would find another way to end their life. Surprisingly, this was not the case.

What actually happened is the suicide rate plummeted from 120 per million people in 1960 to approximately 75 per million in 1970. That is nearly a 40% decrease. If we remember that 44% of the suicides in the country previously used town gas as their method of choice, we realize the drop in the suicide rate coincides almost perfectly with the removal of the town gas.

That means those people did not find another way - they overwhelmingly chose life. Gladwell suggests suicide is coupled, or directly connected, to an individual's preferred method.

Gladwell stated, "If suicide is coupled, then it isn't simply the act of depressed people, it's the act of depressed people at a particular moment of extreme vulnerability and in combination with a readily available lethal means" (2019). The case study presented shows the occurrence of suicide drastically increasing when town gas was introduced into homes, and then the rates falling at nearly the exact percentage once town gas was replaced with natural gas. The people did not find another way, they just did not attempt suicide. When the convenient method was removed, the people chose to live.

Coupling theory in suicide is not popular amongst mental health professionals. It is difficult for people who have spent so much time and effort trying to understand the complexities of the human mind to believe that it's possible to reduce or dissuade suicidal behavior simply by removing the chosen method for it. According to the Center for Disease Control and Prevention, in the United States, handguns are the most frequently used method of suicide (CDC, 2020). The use of a handgun is almost twice as popular as suffocation and almost four times as popular as poisoning (CDC, 2000). For the police population this is no different, the handgun, specifically the officer's duty weapon, is the suicide method of choice.

To further explore the concept of coupling with suicide in an American context, Gladwell presents research on people who tried to jump from the Golden Gate Bridge in San Francisco. Selecting a population from America might be a more applicable comparison to our modern police culture than what was happening in 1960's England. At minimum, it is worth taking a look.

Psychologist Richard Sidon identified 515 individuals who attempted suicide by jumping from the bridge but had their attempt thwarted by some method of intervention. These are persons who went to the bridge to commit suicide but were stopped before they jumped. While the data on the type of intervention is not available, we know at least some of these would be jumpers received their intervention from the police. Interesting that their story has found a way into research on police suicide.

How many of these individuals went on to commit suicide through another method? A mere 25. That means fewer than 5% of the people who were intending to commit suicide by jumping from the bridge decided to commit suicide using a different method. The other 490 people who were going to commit suicide by jumping did not go through with it when jumping was removed as an option. More than 95% of these people chose to live! This study strengthened Gladwell's theory of coupling as it relates to suicide.

The Darkening of the Mind

If the coupling theory is true, would requiring officers to leave their duty weapon at the workplace have the potential to reduce suicide rates? Is it possible doing so might reduce police suicides? According to Blue HELP (2019), up to 80% of officers are believed to have taken their lives with their duty weapons. The fix cannot possibly be that simple. The research implications seem too good to be true.

Presenting coupling to police officers is even less popular than presenting it to mental health professionals. Police are very attached to their guns. Many police carry on and off duty. Some officers want to ensure they are prepared to respond in the event they encounter an emergency situation at any point in time. For others it is more about personal protection. After years of carrying, many officers just don't feel safe without a sidearm. The irony of this mindset as it relates to the profession's suicide method of choice cannot be ignored.

Would officers be best served by leaving their duty weapons at work? Is it possible that making handgun access more difficult could be part of the suicide solution? Would ensuring that the weapon is locked and stored responsibly remove what Gladwell refers to as having this suicide method being "readily available"? These are uncomfortable questions we need to start asking.

Remember, the suicide decision is made in a moment of extreme vulnerability. Would having to retrieve a gun locked in a safe be enough to get an officer past that crucial moment? Or would that not be enough? Would the officer just use their off-duty weapon? Coupling suggests they would not. The jumpers did not find another bridge. Future research efforts will have to inform these provocative and unpopular questions. For today, we remain without an answer.

The elevated level of exposure to death and traumatic events seen by emergency responders can influence their perception of death (Boffa et al., 2016). This repeated exposure to violence and traumatic incidents can remove some of the natural aversion most people have in dealing with death and begin to change processes within the brain (Pompili et al., 2013). This is part of the desensitization we discussed in the last chapter.

Death, for police, becomes a part of life. Mystery and fear become removed, and police begin to view death from an emotionally detached perspective. While this is a survival tool police need to maintain composure during the ugliest parts of their day, it is possible this exposure is another piece of the complicated dynamic that may be contributing to the elevated rates of suicide seen among police professionals. Over the course of a career, the average police officer repeatedly sees accidents, violence, and self-harm. This is creating a problem.

Like any other matter, with repetition comes comfort. The brain begins to process death as just another thing that happens. As we see additional suicides, suicide becomes just another way people die. If we are not careful, after repeated exposure, instead of seeing the devastation and pain the suicide has caused, we might find ourselves almost understanding why the person chose this method of death. This is a very dangerous place for the human psyche to be. It means it now has found a space where suicide is an acceptable option. It is not far from here where it could become an option for you.

If you can remember situations where you thought the suicide you handled "made sense", please check yourself. Your brain has started on a journey to a very dark place. It might be time for you to start talking about some of the darker things you have seen to ensure your thought process surrounding suicide has not become concerning. Suicide should never be viewed as an acceptable option.

Calling for Backup

One of the first things we need to do is see how our current behaviors are contributing to this growing problem. Police must realize they have an inherent reluctance to ask for help. This may be tied to the concept of perceived burdensomeness. More than recognizing this, police professionals need to understand this as a problem. Asking for help is an officer safety skill you must master. If someone is shooting at you, I guarantee you know how to call it out over the radio so you can get some backup. Maybe we need a ten-code for matters of psychological distress.

As is the case with many other areas of human behavior, asking for help gets easier each time a person does it. Asking for help is like public speaking or learning to play an instrument - practice makes perfect. If police professionals can learn to ask for help from others in small areas that do not create a significant sense of vulnerability, then they might have an easier time asking for help when they truly need it. This is a simple process but, like most things presented in this book, it takes intentional action to put it into practice and start to build this skill.

For example, try asking a friend to help you with a home repair. Many jobs are easier with a second set of hands. The practice of asking for assistance in small, non-critical situations can help you build the habit to ask for help when life gets complicated. With intentional placement of asking for assistance combined with repetition (you must do it repeatedly), you will begin to become more comfortable asking friends and family for help. If this habit becomes a normal part of your comfort zone, you are more likely to use it when you find yourself facing an issue that causes you to feel vulnerable.

Avoid Isolation

In approaching the universal human need for belonging, the best thing police can do is to ensure they do not isolate themselves as a method of coping with stress. Often police are so psychologically strained from the pressures of the job that they tend to seek alone time at the end of the day to try to decompress. In doing so, police begin to create a dynamic where they have a limited number of defining relationships. These are the close personal relationships that give us a sense of connection and belonging.

The fewer meaningful connections you have, the more significance each individual relationship holds. The more significant each relationship, the greater the potential impact that relationship has on the officer's sense of self. If we have too few of these connections and one becomes compromised, the results can be devastating.

By learning to intentionally create connections and cultivate friendships, police can ensure they have a wide social network to rely on. This is done by intentionally scheduling time to nurture these relationships. Investing time in relationships is an incredibly important part of maintaining healthy social connections. Often this means sticking to those obligations even when you feel depleted after shift. Social connections take away some of the power of thwarted belonging by intentionally creating multiple situations that include a sense of significance. Building new friendships helps to foster that belonging and focus on the interconnectedness of the individual.

Talk About Suicide

Law enforcement professionals must start openly talking about suicide at the early stages of officers' careers. Police need to recognize the occupational factors that might be contributing to our professions higher rates of suicide and stop pretending they don't exist. We need to know the desensitization to death an officer will eventually experience has the potential to fundamentally change the way they view death and dying. This creates a risk factor if suicide becomes something the officer begins to view as an acceptable option.

The amount of suicide we are exposed to is not healthy for the human psyche. Police need to truly understand when we see others exercise suicide as an option, we should be reminding ourselves this is never an acceptable choice. If we are not mindful, suicide can begin to seem like a less taboo option for us. We must proactively and intentionally protect ourselves from that distorted thinking by keeping it in perspective.

Emphasize the Need for Quality Sleep

The importance of sleep was already discussed as it relates to stress management and overall health. A significant lack of sleep can greatly affect a police officer's ability to think through the long-term impacts of decisions. The world of profit-driven marketing has long understood the link between lack of sleep and impulsivity. (Just look at all the infomercials on in the middle of the night!) This is because as the brain fatigues, the decision-making process becomes compromised (King, 2017). When this happens, we make decisions based on what feels good in the moment. We do not think about the long-term impact or consequences our decision might have. Clearly the implications this type of fatigue-influenced, compromised decision making can have on suicide are easy to identify.

To complicate these matters, remember many police get a rush from the adrenaline released during high risk activities. In a weakened moment, the thrill of doing something dangerous might have more appeal when we combine our compromised decision making with our adrenaline-seeking tendencies. Add alcohol to the mix and the ability to make good decisions becomes almost non-existent. Establishing healthy sleep habits is one way we can protect ourselves from taking the first step down this this dangerous path.

Helpful or Harmful

Police must also be honest about the role our duty weapon plays in officer suicide. If the theory of coupling applies to the suicidal impulses of police officers, then we need to start looking at workplace handgun storage as a potential piece of the solution. More than that, we need to equip our officers with other, healthier tools they can access in that moment of vulnerability, just as easily as they can access their gun.

From peer support programs that include online access and real-time support, to the preventive initiatives that make the occurrence of that critical moment less likely to happen, we need to start looking at suicide as an officer safety issue that needs to be trained for. While no one method provides the solution we need, understanding suicide and adopting healthy habits can help protect ourselves from the threat of suicide we see in the law enforcement profession.

It is likely our solution will be a combination of the methods discussed in this chapter and other interventions that have yet to be discovered as our understanding of this area continues to develop. Despite all the options presented to help lessen the likelihood of suicide, none of these are sure-fire ways to stop suicide. There is only one way to ensure our law enforcement suicides stop. It is time to focus on the individual rather than trying to fix the profession.

A Call to Action

Suicide in law enforcement can no longer be viewed strictly as a mental health issue. It is time police begin to realize otherwise psychologically healthy law enforcement professionals are choosing suicide as an option. We need to understand why this is happening and what we can do to stop it. It is time to act.

While any single officer may not have the ability to stop suicides in our profession, by following the aforementioned action items, each individual officer has the power to stop themselves from becoming part of this problem. I challenge you to become part of the solution today. If every officer reading this book made a commitment to their partner, spouse, or friend that suicide will not be an option for them, we would start to see a change. Furthermore, if each of those officers challenged just ten of their friends to do the same, we would start a movement that just might eradicate suicide in our profession.

Each individual officer has the power to protect himself or herself from the threat of suicide, but it takes intentional action. It requires for us to get used to being uncomfortable and start having courageous conversations. Today is the day for the law enforcement profession to begin moving in the directing of finding a solution...one officer at a time.

Say it loud and proud:

Suicide will never be an option for me.

Chapter 5: Building Psychological Fitness

"You'll never change your life until you change something you do daily. The secret of your success is found in your daily routine." - **John C. Maxwell**

- Understand how to acquire and build psychological fitness in police professionals
- Explore the correlation between physical fitness and psychological wellness
- Learn how physical fitness and psychological wellness have a direct impact on officer safety

Fit for Duty

When it comes to physical fitness and tactical skill level, we know we need to take daily action to keep ourselves in shape. We receive the message constantly from media outlets and from the tragic stories of officers injured in the line-of-duty. If we do not keep ourselves in good physical shape, we have less of a chance of emerging as a survivor if we are part of a violent encounter. Our skills with our tools must be proficient to ensure we can use these tools effectively if we need to protect our lives or the life of another. Unfortunately, the messages to keep ourselves psychologically fit are not communicated to us in the same way or with the same frequency.

Mention psychological resilience to the modern police professional, and you will most likely be met with an eye roll. For some reason, the law enforcement profession insists that resilience should be some type of instinctual skill. Something that is hardwired rather than something that needs to be learned and developed. This could not be further from the truth.

We already discussed how meditation and mindfulness training can be used to build psychological resiliency. These and other stress management techniques are sets of skills that need to be trained, developed, and maintained if you expect to use them effectively in a time of emergency.

Believing these are God-given skills that will miraculously snap into action if needed is an error in critical thinking. It is this reactive approach to stress management that has gotten the police profession into the situation we are in, with too many of our brothers and sisters being affected with depression, anxiety, and addiction. It is time for every officer to step up and make a change. We need to understand that psychological fitness is an essential component of officer safety.

Stress management is an often-overlooked skill that has the potential to help keep officers psychologically strong. Since police professionals are so accustomed to responding to truly high-stress situations, they discount the power of the small annoyances to create a stress reaction in their bodies.

They think if they can effectively manage the "real emergencies" they see at work, then the stuff happening in the station or in their homes should not be issues they struggle with. This misunderstanding is compromising our ability to see the negative impact small stressors can have on our overall psychological health.

Often large-scale stressors are easier to manage effectively because we have developed skill sets specifically designed to handle these situations. We are mindful in our actions as emergency response almost always requires the officer's immediate and complete attention. Even the smallest police agencies usually handle emergencies with some sense of teamwork, helping to ensure everyone is working together for a successful resolution. If the situation is truly distressing, there is often a debriefing of the incident, which can help the officer process the experience in a healthy way. All these strategies come together to help us process emergency situations in a psychologically healthy way.

These details: training, teamwork and talking about what happened are what I like to call the three T's of effective stress management for police. When we approach our known stressors by training for them, working together to find the best solution and talking about what happened, we process our stress in a healthy way. It is the small stressors that we usually do not pay much attention to that start to wear officers down. We think because there is no physical threat to our safety these stressors do not have the capacity to cause any harm. We assume we can just push these issues aside and move past them. We believe if we ignore the issue it will just go away. Failing to address issues in real time can lessen an officer's overall ability to effectively manage stress and lead to long term negative consequences.

Intentionally Creating Resiliency

Stress management comes in many forms and can look different for everyone. While we discussed stress management as a general principal in the first chapter, it is important we take a closer look to truly understand how stress management can cultivate psychological resiliency. With a variety of stress-management options available, how can we find the stress-management tools that meet our needs? There is no right or wrong answer. Each of us must select the stress management approach that works best for who we are as individuals.

We might find a certain approach to stress management effective in one situation and another technique helpful in dealing with a different kind of stress. For example, a vigorous workout might help us get over the frustration we experience when the Sergeant takes away our discretion and directs our actions on a call. This is an aggressive approach used to manage frustration associated with being disrespected. Just because a solid workout can help us manage the internal stress that comes from within our organization, this does not mean it is the only stress management technique we need to learn.

That same workout might not be as effective in managing the stress of a situation where we see a disturbing crime scene involving people who lost their lives. For this we might require a different strategy to help us manage the stress associated with this situation. A less aggressive option, like debriefing with a co-worker or engaging peer support, might be a better fit. For this reason, it makes sense for the law enforcement professional to understand a wide variety of stress-management techniques. That way we have several options to choose from. This is necessary considering the wide variety of stressful situations that modern police encounter.

As we explore the stress management techniques this book describes and the reasons they work, we should be able to identify several methods that will work for us in different situations. It is important that the stress management techniques we select feel comfortable for us as individuals. If they do not feel comfortable today, we might have to apply intentional action to build our comfort level. Many of these things can be practiced indiscreetly as part of our daily routine to build our skill. This practice will ensure proficiency will be there in the event of an emergency.

Remember, these are not tactics we can read about one time and then expect to pluck out of thin air when we need them. By incorporating these techniques into our daily habits, we will create an environment where we are intentionally and proactively managing stress. This will build our psychological fitness and make it less likely we will suffer one of the negative consequences of poor stress management. Once we've done this, we will find ourselves functioning as a skilled tactician when that inevitable high-stress day finds you. We will become Jedi Masters of stress.

Things We Cannot Ignore

The mind cannot ignore what the body is doing. Exercise can do so much more for a person than just keep them physically fit. Scientific studies on the benefits of exercise include not only physical strength, but also cardiovascular health and positive psychological impact. In fact, research suggests aerobic exercise, which improves cardiorespiratory fitness, is an effective treatment for PTS, depression, and anxiety. Research shows exercise may be comparable or superior to other common treatments, such as psychotherapy and pharmacology (Helburg, Hayes & Hayes, 2019). This is a potentially game changing find for the police profession. Exercise should be a mandate, not just an option. If we are going to survive in a profession as physically and psychologically demanding as police work, a regular exercise routine is essential.

There are many misconceptions about exercise and the amount and type required to receive the benefits needed. When we have a better understanding of how exercise affects the inner workings of the body, we will be able to make an informed choice about what type of exercise is right for you. I am not suggesting that any of us need to start training with the intensity of an Olympic athlete, but I am stating from both a physical and psychological wellness perspective; exercise needs to be a part of every healthy police officers daily routine.

Often, we think of exercise as it relates to fitness from a physical perspective - we think of the magazines with the muscle-bound men and women on the cover. These images condition us to think that health and fitness directly relate to body fat percentage. Truth be told, muscle mass is only part of a much larger fitness picture.

Certainly, your body mass index (BMI) has a correlation to your health, but you might be surprised at what a person with a healthy BMI actually looks like. It often does not look like those people who grace the cover of the fitness magazines. They often have a BMI that is well below the "healthy range." I am not saying these people are unhealthy, but that fitness does not have to take a muscle-bound form. It is time we start being honest about what responsible fitness does and does not look like, especially from a practical police perspective.

Speaking of a practical police perspective, police work has very unique physical demands. We need to take these demands into consideration when we commit to an exercise routine. Not all exercise is created equal and not all exercise strategies will help us prepare for the unique demands of our profession. We need to look at what type of fitness is needed for law enforcement and understand how we can use exercise to best prepare ourselves for our job. Exercise should be looked at as physical fitness training for police work. Out daily fitness routine should prepare us to perform as we may be called to do in emergency situations.

For too many years, my exercise routine was comprised of 30 minutes of cardio and 30 minutes of strength training. While this is not the worst exercise model, I was approaching the cardio component all wrong. I was running for distance and speed rather than doing interval training. If you think about what our job demands of us, you will quickly see the error of my ways. When was the last time any cop you know was in a 30 minute foot-pursuit?

As I continued to research exercise-science and reflect on what cops were actually called to do, it was clear the best way to prepare myself for the demands of the street was high-intensity-interval-training (HIIT). This is an exercise strategy that alternates periods of short, intense anaerobic exercise with longer aerobic exercise recovery segments. During HIIT, we intentionally spike our heart-rate and get close to maximum performance, then slow it down and catch our breath. Then we do it again. Through adoption of this training strategy we can best prepare ourselves for the demands of our profession.

Think about what we do on the street. Whether a physical altercation, a foot-pursuit or an emergency call response, we go from zero to one hundred and back to zero again in rapid succession. HIIT will prepare us for those intense periods of high-physical demand and the associated rapid increase in heart rate followed by the eventual slowdown we see on the street. So many officers have suffered cardiac incidents after being exposed to situations with these dynamics. If we could get law enforcement to start training like this across the board, we would see less heart-attacks after these types of incidents. As the old saying goes, "we need to train as if our life depends on it"… because it does!

Hopefully you are familiar with HIIT and are using it as part of your current exercise routine. If not, please do some research and explore the benefits high-intensity-interval-training might have for you. Beginning to incorporate HIIT segments into your regular exercise routine just might save your life.

Fitness Standards and Your Health

We all know the male versus female struggle with the fitness screening in our profession. I am going to be speaking in generalizations here, so if you are a person who does not fit the stereotype I am referring to, please know that effective officers come in all shapes and sizes. In no way is it my intent to make this discussion offensive or exclusive. I am attempting to provide this information in the most comprehensive way possible to facilitate depth of understanding for those who might not have a knowledge base in this area.

For the more than two decades I have been a police officer. During this time, I have seen the same pattern repeat itself. When we get to physical fitness testing, as a rule, women struggle with the bench press and men struggle with the lower back flexibility. No test is going to be able to measure all the capabilities needed to perform the job of police officer due to the unpredictable nature of the streets. These screenings have been designed by experts to assess general fitness. They are being used across the country and are intended to measure abilities for strength, cardiovascular fitness, and flexibility on a generalized scale.

Some agencies continue to conduct fitness testing for police throughout their careers. This is an excellent habit. If you are working for an agency that requires fitness testing on a regular basis, I hope you appreciate this for what it is - a proactive effort on the part of your agency to keep the team members healthy and happy.

All too often when an agency has annual testing, the officers spend their time resenting the test rather than preparing for it. I have listened to officers across the nation complain about how the job wants them to maintain fitness but will not pay for gym memberships or allow them to work out on duty. I agree that agencies should consider fitness to be so important that they are willing to provide these things for their officers. Unfortunately, I can agree all I want, but unless I am your chief (and I am not), then wishing things were different does not change reality. We need to stop complaining and rise above this. We need to take ownership for our fitness whether our agency is providing us with the time and tools needed to support our fitness or not.

I have spoken with hundreds of chiefs on this topic. There are many reasons why offering gym memberships or allowing for working out on duty are not possible for their agencies. At times, the chief is supportive, but the political environment does not allow these practices for whatever reason. Other times, there is the opinion that the officer was fit when hired, so maintaining that fitness is an expected part of the job. Reasons and excuses do not really matter. As a profession, fitness is not something we can sacrifice.

Fitness is essentially important—not just for professional performance, but also for the officer's overall health and quality of life. It is time we stop being so stubborn. We must stop behaving like victims of situations beyond our control. The complaining about what is not provided for us must stop. We need to come together and take the matter of our personal fitness into our own hands.

Practicing self-care habits has far reaching benefits. An individual who is taking good care of his or her physical health is most likely also bringing a higher level of attention to their psychological wellness. In part, this may be because exercise has such tremendous stress management benefits. Additionally, taking care of our bodies can have a holistic impact. An individual who puts continual proactive effort into being strong enough for the job usually does not limit their effort to just the physical body. Self-care, including a regular exercise routine, is an important first step in building psychological strength.

Workouts are not easy. Often the mental effort it takes to get into the gym and get through a workout is more of a challenge than the actual physical effort. Officers who incorporate exercise as part of their self-care routine know this profession can and will present physical challenges that they must be prepared to face. What they might not know is that the physical exercise they are engaging in has as much of a psychological benefit as a physical one. They are building strength of both the body and the mind. Officers who commit to regular exercise are better prepared to handle both the physical and psychological threats of the law enforcement profession.

Positive Leads to More Positive

In the agencies that do provide benefits such as the ability to work out on shift, paid gym memberships, and a culture that prioritizes physical fitness, most officers thrive. Healthy officers are more likely to be happy officers, and happy officers are less likely to be injured on duty. When we take the time out of our day to work out, we often make better food choices throughout that day. As an additional benefit, in the evenings or whenever we are sleeping (damn shift work!), we are more likely to be physically tired and experience a higher quality of sleep.

Sleeping more, exercising regularly, and eating better - sounds like the perfect proactive stress management approach. As a bonus, on-duty fitness programs create better overall health for the officers. Agencies who make the decision to support fitness initiatives often know the result is happier healthier workers. A culture of fitness benefits both the employer and the employee.

Increasing levels of physical activity are proven to have a positive impact on an individual's physical health and mental well-being. Physical activity is also known to influence work-related issues such as a lower rate of sickness absence and reduced insurance premiums (Amlani & Munir, 2014). This results in a cost savings for the agency. A work environment that places an emphasis on personal wellbeing can also lead to a higher level of morale (Davis, 2014). If you have spent any time working as part of a police agency, you know firsthand the powerful impact the morale of the troops can have on daily operations. As you can see, investing in officer health and wellness not only benefits the officer, but has significant benefits for the agency.

Another important area of consideration is how health and happiness correlate. Happy officers, like happy people, deliver a higher quality of work performance. Research shows a happy brain performs up to 30% more efficiently than a brain that is negative, neutral, or stressed (Acher, 2010). Better performance results in more productivity and fewer mistakes. This can create fewer instances of use of force and lessened liability for the agency. Some agencies see the potential for the financial savings to be so significant, they even offer wellness incentives to motivate officers to participate.

While incentives such as stipends or additional time off can provide motivation for police to commit to fitness, as a profession we need to find ways to motivate officers toward a higher level of fitness whether an incentive exists or not. Sure, the benefits of fitness create better job performance, but they also create a better quality of life. The increase in health benefits, energy levels and psychological resiliency that comes from an active lifestyle should be motivation enough for all of us to commit to improved fitness today. It is time we take action. We need to come together and commit to fitness as part of our professional standard. More importantly, each of us as individual officers need to commit to remain physically fit during the course of our career.

The stress of a law enforcement profession will compromise both the human body and mind if we allow it to happen. A commitment to fitness is one of the simplest things we can do to ensure we remain both mentally and physically healthy during the course of our career. When this is done, we will start to see our longevity rates rise as our prevalence of disease rapidly decreases. It is time for us to be the change. It is time we get serious about our health.

Chapter 6: Wellness, Success, and Motivation

"Failure isn't fatal, but failure to change might be."

- John Wooden

- Explore the aspects of a comprehensive officer wellness initiative
- Learn how to move from policy to practice in creating a culture of wellness
- Understand human motivation and how to leverage it within your organization

The Importance of Healthy Police

I remember one of my first exposures to creating an officer wellness initiative. The decision makers noticed that several officers in their agency had become out of shape. This concern was real, it was not about sloppy appearance in uniform. Lack of fitness was a serious issue in this agency. The administration realized something needed to be done.

Through regular and innocent department conversations, several officers had shared information about health issues such as high cholesterol and high blood pressure. Now, we all know personal medical information is private. That is, unless you go around telling everyone about it. As a general rule, cops are terrible at keeping secrets.

The issues went deeper than that, though. At defensive tactics training, some officers were unreasonably winded. Other officers had a difficult time getting up after ground-fighting drills. These are serious issues. If you cannot get up after being knocked down in training, how are you going to get up if this happens on the street?

Due to several members of the team exhibiting these and other health concerns, the well-intentioned administration decided to implement fitness testing for the first time in the agency's history. They formed a committee and came up with a plan. Meeting upon meeting was held to work out all the details. As I am sure you can imagine, when the time came to implement the program, it was a total disaster.

The Fitness Testing Controversy

In the planning stages, I was fortunate enough to have a seat at the table as the administration discussed implementing annual fitness testing. The idea was to use the same test that was used for hiring, which allowed for variations of performance based on age and gender. They discussed requiring all officers to participate in the test, without consequence, to establish a baseline. Once the baseline fitness level for each officer was established, intervention with those officers needing to improve their fitness would commence.

One of the first steps was the establishment of a program to help officers who were not at the acceptable standard get to a healthier place. Officers who needed assistance would receive personal training and health coaching. This would be provided by members of the agency trained with fitness as a specialty area and the intervention would take place on duty. This agency also discussed giving the officers a very realistic timeline to achieve their goals, allowing two years to help build fitness levels back up to standard. Ultimately, if the individual officers did not get themselves up to the acceptable level, progressive discipline would begin.

A tentative date for the initial round of testing was set. The baseline would be established soon. It was a good plan, and everyone at the table was very happy. Or so they thought...

Before the meeting adjourned, I gently mentioned to the less-than-fit-looking administrators at the table that if they were going to mandate the troops take the test, then they should lead by example and plan to take the test as well. Not too surprisingly, the tone of the room shifted immediately. The plan no longer looked as reasonable as it had moments before. While the idea seemed generous when applied to their expectations of other people, when they considered the plan for themselves, the requirements suddenly seemed a little too aggressive.

While nobody spoke the words aloud at the table that day, I believe there was also an ego component involved in the reconsideration. In that moment, they had to assess their personal fitness levels. When was the last time they had gotten out and run a 5K, or even the mile and a half they would be asking the officers to do? Were they in the habit of lifting weights or doing push-ups? And what had sitting at a desk for the last ten years done to the flexibility of their lower back? Would they ever be able to get to the point where they were up to standard in that area? These very quickly became real questions and concerns.

Eventually the agency did establish a wellness program, but it looked different than the original plan. Instead of starting in three months, the launch was pushed out a year. The standard screening test required participants to run, but they decided to allow an option for officers to walk a longer distance if they preferred (guess which option most of the administrators selected). This was done in line with the fitness program another local agency was using (seemingly effectively) to accommodate officers with serious health issues. The new test design also allowed for a medical exemption provision that was not previously considered. A doctor could write a note excusing an officer from all or some of the portions of the assessment. This would allow individual officers to not have to meet the requirement in certain areas with a medical excuse. It is amazing how quickly things change when you are no longer imposing standards on others, and you are now requiring them of yourself.

I would love to report that the program was a success. Unfortunately, I am unable to do so.

Epic Fail

The people who were in good shape were insulted that such a watered-down version of the test was offered. They were flat-out pissed off. In fact, many of those who could have easily passed the test by the standards set for a 20-year-old instead decided to put in the least effort possible. Some of them even decided to walk instead of run, despite the fact their current level of fitness would never require them to choose this as an option.

Some of the most fit members of the agency, guys and gals who would push their physical abilities to the limit in the gym, did the bare minimum the day of the fitness assessment in attempt to prove a point.

If an officer selected the walk option, it was a three-mile course. This would have been tedious to do on a track, where the run was usually conducted, so administrators established a course through the streets of the community. Believe it or not, some of the officers (not the fit ones) were caught cheating to improve their time on the three-mile walk. Because a route monitor was not positioned on every corner, there were unintentional opportunities for shortcuts—and some officers exploited them. It's difficult to explain why an officer would cheat on a fitness test designed to keep them healthy, but I'm telling you it happened. You can't make this shit up.

And the officers who could not pass the test? They were embarrassed. This embarrassment heightened as administrators assigned them to work with one of their peers—often less senior than they were—as a fitness coach. While the in-house fitness coaches were intended to protect the ego of the officers needing fitness intervention, it had the opposite effect.

For several years, the program ran as designed. When a new chief came in, the program was reevaluated. When it was found to not be making the progress intended, the program was abandoned.

I offer you this example to prove one point. From a behavioral science perspective, we know there is an effective way to modify human behavior and an ineffective way. Human behavior is simply not modified through punishment or threat of punishment. You may achieve compliance, but your subjects' behavior patterns will not change.

So, if punishments do not work to motivate people, what does? If you want to motivate people to change their behaviors, you must give them an incentive or a positive reward. The question then becomes, what is an effective incentive to get officers to invest effort into improving their personal fitness level? You would think the improved health, additional energy and increased psychological resiliency we discussed in the last chapter would be motivation enough, but sadly, for many officers it is not. These officers often want financial incentives and time compensation. This should make us take a long hard look at our priorities. Which is more important to us... long-term improvements in health or a little extra cash?

Successful Efforts Abound

Fortunately, far more frequent than stories of failure are the stories of successful fitness programs. One agency successfully implemented a meditation and yoga program and are seeing amazing results. A member of this agency sat in a training course with me last year, and afterwards, I spoke with him to ask about the details of the program. Being a yoga instructor for the past eighteen years, I wanted to know how his agency got the officers to participate. He told me it was simple - the union had negotiated a schedule that allowed for a shift overlap.

The spirit of this overlap was to allow time for physical fitness, training initiatives, and information sharing between shifts. The agency had been tracking how sports teams were using a regular yoga practice to help reduce injury in their players (Capouya, 2003), and the administration wondered if they could use this same strategy to help protect their officers from injury.

The administrators decided to design a program to expose the officers to yoga. They knew from the studies with professional sports teams that once the players start doing yoga, they would experience such a measurable benefit from yoga that they would stay committed to continuing to practice. These professional athletes not only saw improvements in their physical performance with an active yoga practice, but they also reported enhanced mental focus. If this could work for athletes, why couldn't it work for officers? The agency decided to give it a try.

At this agency, the officers learned they would be starting their shift in workout gear. When they arrived for roll call, a professional yoga instructor greeted them and took the officers through an introduction to yoga and a basic class. That was it. No discussion, no pre-planning, no opportunity for resistance, no opt out. All the officers on shift took the class.

Unlike many other exercise disciplines, yoga can be modified to accommodate every fitness level and body type. The class was offered consistently as part of the weekly routine, and after a few classes, the officers started to feel better. They discussed this experience with genuine surprise and disbelief. The officers could feel the intervention working. The officers who were scheduled to take the class started to tell other officers about their experience. Interest in the class increased as the word of the mental and physical health benefits spread throughout the agency.

The class is still offered to this day. The officers attend voluntarily through a sign-up process. This class is one of the many fitness options now available. Some attend as part of their shift, and others come in to take the class during their time off. The officers who take the class on their time off are not paid, and they don't complain. They see a benefit in not having to pay a fee for the class as they would at a yoga studio or fitness center. At some point, they know they will get their chance to attend on shift. When that happens, their fellow officers might come in on their time off to join them. Officers on this agency workout together. It is something they do. It has become part of their culture; a culture that invests in the health of their officers. A culture that understands officer wellness is an essential component of officer safety.

Motivation and Daily Action

In this agency, officers do not pursue fitness because the agency is making them. They do it because participating in the program makes them feel better. This is an example of what true motivation looks like. It is the missing piece the mandatory fitness programs lacked. It is a completely different way of achieving a change in behavior. It also shows that habits change through daily action, not through a once-a-year mandatory participation requirement.

Police, being skeptical in nature, often think wellness programs are some type of Big Brother attempt to gain personal information to later be used against them. I'm not saying officers are paranoid, but if you recall the chapter about the psychological testing, you should remember skepticism is one of the areas the police profile produces an elevated result.

There are police officers out there who know they need to get in shape and are doing nothing about it. Some of those officers work for agencies that offer wellness programs that would help them. Yet, these officers continue to remain in a state of compromised wellness because they chose to allow ridiculous conspiracy theories to stop them from taking advantage of these offerings. When police professionals think like this, we become our own worst enemies.

If you know someone who might need some help in recommitting to fitness, it is my hope this chapter inspired you to be a motivating factor in that person's life. Remember, it is going to be difficult for them to ask for help. You might see better results if you make the first move. Inviting this person to hit the gym with you after shift or even train for a local 5K for charity may be the opportunity this person has been waiting for. Sharing experiences of how your sleep improved after starting to work out regularly or talking about how much better you feel on the days you work out would be a great place to start.

More importantly than motivating others, is ensuring you retain your commitment to fitness yourself. Make sure you are not one of the people making excuses. For far too long, I allowed a moderate level of fitness to be good enough for me. Now that I have recommitted to working out, I cannot believe I was ever so foolish. The energy, clarity, and reduction of stress I realize on the days I work out are my true motivators. Knowing that I am growing stronger and more resilient are a bonus.

Committing to improving your health through fitness does not have to be an expensive endeavor. The nation is full of full-service fitness centers offering memberships for as low as $10 a month. Head outdoors to take a walk or go for a run and you double down on your wellness benefits by adding a dose of nature to your workout. If you are more the inside type, some burpees, body weight exercises or a simple set of suspension straps can provide you with almost unlimited options to make strength training possible in virtually any setting. No matter what you choose to do, do something. This is a profession where fitness for duty is a requirement. It is time we start taking a proactive approach to our personal wellness to ensure we lead by example.

Chapter 7: Overcoming Resistance

"He that is good for making excuses is seldom good for anything else." - **Benjamin Franklin**

- Understand self-sabotage and how it occurs
- Explore factors that negatively impact human motivation and how they might be impacting your organization
- Learn to overcome the cult of the average and rise above mediocracy

The Enemy Within

On the street, we have no problem helping to keep our fellow officers safe. We back up our shift partners (even the ones we don't like) and we help officers from other agencies we've never even met. Today, officer safety is one of our primary concerns. We need to take our same commitment to tactical safety and bring it to the locker room as well. It's time we realize only a small percentage of the threats to our safety happen on the street. Most of our safety threats lie with the compromised physical and psychological wellness we see in our profession. The power to address these safety threats lie in the self-care decisions we make everyday.

Recently I was at an employee wellness meeting as an observer. This company, for the first time, was offering its employee base, police officers included, a wellness incentive. The company requested voluntary participation in a wellness monitoring program. No exercise, no diet, no effort—the employee simply had to participate in a screening that measured a few areas that wellness experts believed to be important to personal health. The areas being measured were body-mass index (BMI), nicotine usage (through a saliva swab test), cholesterol (finger stick), and heart recovery rate. All participants, regardless of their wellness assessment, would receive a monthly financial incentive for participation. With improved scoring, the dollar amount of the monthly payment went up.

When it was time for questions, the audience response was quite entertaining. People wanted to know what was being done with the DNA collected for the nicotine screening after the testing. The poor civilian presenter had no idea what the police officer was asking. He asked for clarification. He explained the results were delivered immediately and the participant was informed on the spot. I believe the program administrator believed the question was about protection of privacy. The police officer continued to ask if the DNA profile was captured and how it was stored. He wanted to know if it was put into a database, and if so, what the database was used for?

The presenter did not understand the police mindset. He explained it was a foam swab that was tested for the presumptive presence of nicotine and that the swab was placed into the garbage after the test. It was placed into the garbage in front of the participant. No storage, no database, no conspiracy.

I know not every police officer is paranoid, but that elevated profile impacts some of our police professionals more than others. I'm willing to bet you know a guy or gal in your agency who would have a similar stream of questions. If you still don't know what I am talking about, please pay attention. That paranoid person might be you.

I have seen agencies where these fitness benefits are offered, but for some reason, officers still choose not to take advantage of the opportunities. I know of agencies that offer a health club membership, and only about 25% of the officers in the agency use it. When asked why, the officers stated after their shift they had other obligations and were not able to spend time working out.

In response and in hopes of greater participation of officers using the health club benefits, the agency changed the policy and allowed officers to work out for a specified amount of time during their shift. Still, the number of officers using the workout facility did not change. Now time was not the issue, the agency was perplexed. Officers were surveyed to understand why they were not taking advantage of the workout benefits. In this situation the agency recognized that officer wellness was an essential component of officer safety, but the officer's themselves were failing to see it.

These were the officers who had previously been complaining about gym membership costs not being covered by the agency. The same officers that complained about lack of time to devote to fitness outside of shift hours. But when those obstacles were removed, the officers were still not working out.

Some officers stated they didn't want to get sweaty during their shift (showers were provided). Other officers didn't want to expend their energy on exercise in case they were called to task during their shift (science shows exercise increases energy instead of depleting it). Still others came up with other excuses ranging from questions about injury liability to a concern about hairstyle appearance after a workout (again- can't make it up). The excuses may have been abundant, but the real reason was the same. These officers did not understand that their health was directly related to their ability to be safe in this profession.

The time for excuses is over. Too many police are dying because of things we can control. We talk about how the suicide rate and occupational association to chronic disease are unacceptable, but we are failing to do anything about it. If we want different results, we need to start taking different action. The excuse creating in our profession will continue as long as we allow it. It's time we start asking ourselves why we are working so hard to create excuses and what, if anything, we can do to change it.

Resistance and Mediocrity

The concept of resistance is one that has been deeply explored outside of the field of police work (Robbins, 2017). This is because resistance affects all human beings…if we let it. It's a natural occurrence that will keep us from becoming the best version of ourselves. It is important for police to understand because it is often the factor that is keeping us stuck in our old destructive habits.

While physics tells us a body in motion stays in motion, it appears the opposite is also true. A body at rest will stay at rest—that is, until it's forced into motion. The key is for all of us to find a way to get through the psychological resistance associated with change, so we can engage in new habits designed to help us achieve our full potential.

The old joke says police officers hate two things: change and the way things currently are. Police are notorious for complaining about the current state of operations. When someone listens to their concerns and takes corrective action, police officers complain even louder about the proposed change.

This is part of what contributes to the police culture's celebration of mediocrity. When someone asks us why we do something a certain way, we answer "we have always done it that way". This is true in both our professional and personal lives. Even the most highly motivated officer can fall prey to the cult of the average. The comfort associated with complacency is simply intoxicating.

Mindset is Everything

Officers start this job full of excitement and energy for the work they have been hired to do. In fact, most new officers cannot even believe someone is paying them to do such a cool job. They go out there and give it their all. They pull cars over, find bad guys, and make good arrests.

Then, somewhere along the line, something shifts. This young, motivated officer starts to get feedback from other members of the team—sometimes even from their supervisors – telling them to slow down. How many times have senior officers said in the halls of police departments across the nation, "it's a marathon rookie, not a sprint"? Seasoned officers accuse young officers of making them "look bad" through proactive enforcement efforts. This type of peer pressure is powerful because it happens in a culture where being a member of a team is essential. Older officers tell new, aggressive officers that the pay is the same no matter how hard they work.

Early on in their careers, the young officers are resilient. They persist in their proactive enforcement efforts. They love the job and want to work. Keeping themselves busy seems to help the time go by. Then, usually about five years or so into a police career, a change happens. Disillusionment sets in. The young officers try for a promotion or specialty assignment, only to have the older officers, the ones doing almost no work, get selected for those positions. The young officers feel like fools. They thought hard work would be rewarded. They were wrong.

So, the young officers become a little salty. They decide to slow down. Not because they gave into the pressure, but just to see if anyone notices. They stop bringing their best self to work each day. They do just enough to keep the Sergeant off their case. This is where the celebration of mediocracy begins.

These officers have just joined the cult of the average. These officers quickly learn that no one misses their professional best. In fact, a few people even congratulate them for finally "figuring it out". What a destructive cycle.

For the rest of these officers' career, they show up to work, stay under the radar, and go home at the end of the day. This becomes the new normal and is repeated day in and day out. When the specialty assignment opens the next time, this officer applies and is accepted. All this is not a result for the time they spent working hard, it is a reward for the time they spend hardly working. Less work for the officer often means less work for the Sergeant. This might mean a better evaluation when it comes time for rankings. After all, it is pretty difficult to make a mistake when you are barely doing anything at all.

One day, that same officer tells a new recruit to slow down and not to work so hard. He has become what he once resisted. He is no longer trying. He is just showing up. He is still getting his paycheck - in fact he still gets his raises. If he sticks around long enough, he might even get promoted. Complacency in action. We see this in agencies across the nation.

Herein lies part of the problem with the police profession. Nowhere in life can you just show up and expect success. When we go to work and our professional model tells us it is enough to just show up, something becomes broken inside of us. Unintentionally, just showing up can become our default method of operation. This is creating huge problems for us in our personal lives.

We start just showing up in other areas. At home, with our spouses and with our children, we just show up. We have no energy, we are not engaged, we put no effort into being our best and we mistakenly think it will be enough. It is not.

Our partners, our families and our children deserve more. Every person who loves a police officer deserve the best version of us in that relationship. We cannot spend all our energy at work resentfully trying to get through another day and have nothing left to give when we get home. When this happens... if it happens... the problems begin. If we forget how to be the best version of ourselves, our relationships suffer and so do we.

If we allow our career to look like this, when we honorably retire, we start to feel like something is missing. We are deeply damaged by the profession, but we do not understand how or why. We have spent twenty-plus years being less than our professional best and it did not serve us well. Deep down inside, resentment sets in. The job has changed us in so many ways. We become bitter as this subconscious knowledge eats away at us. The result is a retired professional who was never asked to live up to their potential. As a consequence, for this life of mediocracy, this retiree is psychologically unwell.

Resisting the Cult of the Average

This does not happen to every officer, but it happens to far too many of us. It is time we take a stand and fight for our profession. The cult of the average does not have to rule the day. Each of us can decide to bring our best to work each day. We can remain engaged in the fascinating career we have been called to. If we are to make this happen, we need to acknowledge that the celebration of mediocracy is not serving us well and we deserve better—both as police officers and as people.

We must decide to not be average, even when we feel external pressures telling us to slow down and not work so hard. Good enough can never be accepted as good enough. We need to mentor younger officers and tell them not to give into a professional life of mediocracy. Each of us must bring the best of ourselves to work each day knowing that habit will encourage us to bring our best back home as well.

This often looks like us working harder than many of those that surround us. We must stop making those comparisons. The Buddhists believe comparison is the root of suffering. It does not matter what other people are doing. We have to start doing what is best for us. Like matters of physical and psychological wellness, we need to lead with the behavior we want to see as the professional standard. We need to be the change.

The para-military construct of the typical police department can cause challenges to those trying to be true to themselves. The limited opportunities for promotion and advancement often create a competitive rather than a cooperative environment. If we are not careful, our efforts at self-improvement might be interpreted as self-promotion. This can be misunderstood by other people and viewed as behavior outside of what is in the best interest of the team. If this happens people will try to undermine you. You will need to be prepared to accept these challenges if you are to continue to be your personal best.

What's a practical way to resist the cult of the average? The answers lie in understanding neuroscience and how to create psychological resiliency.

Chapter 8: Understanding Neuroscience

"I can be changed by what happens to me. But I refuse to be reduced by it." —*Maya Angelou*

- Explore the principles of human instincts and how to leverage them to your advantage
- Understand how perspective influences reality
- Learn how to cultivate resiliency and use it to improve your professional experience

Humanity is Hardwired

By understanding how the brain works and how our behaviors influence our psyche, we can start to live the personal and professional lives we've always imagined. Our brain is constantly taking in all that surrounds us in this world. This amazing organ processes the things we do and see. It's important that we learn a little about the human brain and how it works to ensure we're prepared to meet the psychological demands of this profession.

If you ever get the opportunity to attend a human factors training, I highly recommend you do so. The classes are designed to help you understand how humans are hard-wired to respond to certain stimuli. This is often when our survival instincts take over, and we're compelled to act in ways that are driven by the subconscious.

Human factors training is seldom part of the mandatory training areas we so often see in law enforcement. I would argue it is equally as important as ethics or use of force. In fact, I believe someday academies will begin to teach human factors and psychological resiliency as part of the police basic training model. Through understanding how we are designed to respond as human beings, we can begin to understand why we act the way we do. This is crucially important in understanding the areas of de-escalation and emotional control.

If your agency will not approve this type of training, I recommend finding a way to send yourself. It is that important. If it is not possible for you to get to a training, please go out and buy one of the many books written on the subject. *The Invisible Gorilla and Other Ways Our Intuitions Deceive Us* (Chabris, 2011) or *The Power of Habit: Why We Do What We Do in Life and Business* (Duhigg, 2012) are just two examples of fantastic books that can help you better understand your instinctual responses.

Know Thy Self

Once we understand where our responses stem from, we can begin to consciously decide if those instincts serve us well in our given situation. We may often find they do not.

The structure of our brain has not changed since the beginning of humankind, but society has changed substantially. As police, we need to interpret and evaluate each event against the backdrop of the situation. When our brain interprets the situation as a threat, it may trigger our fight-or-flight response, resulting in some compromised cognitive functioning. It is as important that we understand what is happening on the inside of our bodies as it is that we accurately assess situations we respond to.

We can bring intention to any matter or situation, no matter how strong our instinctual tendency, but it takes dedicated effort to make this happen. Once we are responding intentionally, we are using our instinctive drive to our benefit. Like many things in life, instinctual reactions can be good or bad. If we are paying attention, we can notice what's happening in our bodies and intentionally select our reactions to ensure we are responding in a way appropriate to our current situation.

It is likely you know when your body is dumping adrenaline into your system. This is true even if you have never given it much thought. Many people describe this moment as feeling a rush of energy or a flushing of the face. Others feel constriction in the throat or warmth in the ears. Remember that adrenaline is released from the part of our brain nearest to the brain stem, so it makes sense many of us feel the first effect in that same area of our bodies.

If we know we're dumping adrenaline, also called epinephrine, we can take extra care to ensure our actions are well directed. We know there is a threat (real or perceived), and we are now responding to it. Reactive and proactive cannot exist at the same time, so when our bodies start responding, we need to get in there and be intentional about what is going to happen next. This allows us to be proactive in our approach to managing our natural stress response. If we do not do this, we're going to function in reactive mode.

A recent example of reactive mode was captured in a tragic shooting in an airport not too long ago. The grainy video shows an armed assailant opening fire near the luggage retrieval area and people moving to the side and beginning to lie down. This is an example of what might happen if we are not intentional about directing our action when we begin to experience a stress response. None of those people made a conscious decision about what the best course of action would be. Something was happening in their bodies they were not familiar with. There was obvious danger and they were afraid. The emotional part of their brain took control and the logical decision-making center shut down.

Here those unprepared people stopped and waited to see the impact of the damage before they decide to take action. This is often referred to as fight, flight or freeze. A complete inability of the logical brain to process what is happening causes to take no action. As police, no action is not an acceptable option. That is why we train. We must be prepared to intentionally move ourselves out of that instinctual, primitive human response.

The Destruction of Resilience

Resilience is a fascinating area. The definition of resilience has changed over time, which makes understanding it even more difficult. When I started in this profession, resilience was equated to "suck it up and move on." It was about being able to get over a disappointing event and continue to move forward. The problem with this was most people were faking it. The officers were going through the motions and moving forward as expected, but inside the memories of the situation continued to haunt them.

Officers were continuing to go about their daily routine, but they were stuck psychologically, ruminating on past events. Rumination is where your mind plays a set of circumstances over and over in your head. Sometimes instead of things turning out the way they did, in the replay, things turn out the way you wanted them to be. Other times you just play back the same scenario. This is a natural human tendency, but it does not serve us well. This is especially true if it is not reality based (changed details). Rumination can create an exhausting psychological energy suck and keep the officer from processing what actually happened and finding a resolution.

It is not always a call for service or emergency response that creates this type of psychological sticking point. Over the years, I have met literally hundreds of officers who have admitted to me that they have spent too much time and effort focusing on how unfairly they were treated within their agency.

Here the officers "got over it" from the vantage point of the outside world, meaning they continued to go to work and function as a professional, but inside the officer a storm of anger, resentment, and frustration took hold. This officer was far from over it and it was creating a psychological energy drain that would slowly compromise the officer's ability to handle additional stressful situations.

Mentoring the Next Generation

As a new generation of workers came to join us, mentoring became a common practice in police agencies. Formalized field training programs brought a way for police departments to encourage new officers to learn from their mistakes with the guidance of a senior officer, making sure the mistake was not too serious or dangerous. Slowly the "suck it up, kid" approach was losing its hold and our profession looked like it was headed in a healthier direction.

Mentors taught newer officers to learn a lesson when something difficult or disappointing happened. What once would have been considered a failure was now viewed as a success because the officer learned from the experience. The definition of resilience seemed to morph into "learn something from the experience and keep pushing forward."

In theory, this is a great practice. But even with a mentor, the officer would often become discouraged because the negative event occurred. The mentor would encourage the officer to not focus on the past, but to shake it off and do better next time. While the officer knew they were not supposed to let the experience bother them, somehow the moment was still alive inside their mind. The officer wanted to understand why and how the situation occurred. They wanted to know how they could stop something similar from happening again. The mentor likely tried their best but did not have all the answers the officer needed. This generation of law enforcement officers was taught they were supposed to be moving past it, but despite the mentor's best effort, the officer still felt stuck.

The best way to help this situation is to continue to allow the officer to discuss the details until it is resolved. Often the new officer does not want to bring it up because the mentor's advice was to move past the frustration. The officer feels embarrassed that they are still thinking about it. We need to find a way in our mentoring efforts to address these sticking points and allow for dialogue until the issue is fully resolved.

Expressing frustration verbally or in writing allows the human brain to process upsetting situations. This is why talk therapy works (a deeper discussion on this will be presented in Chapter 11). This is something we need to explain to our FTO's and supervisors. Repetition allows healing to happen. Incorporating intentionally asking about sticking points might be a good place to start. Something like, "Are there any calls we handled or situations we have encountered that are not sitting well with you?" would open that door and allow for a way to have a helpful conversation on an issue already addressed. This is a good practice for supervisors to engage in with employees at all levels. It would ensure officers know they can talk about issues that they are struggling to understand or make sense of.

When Things Do Not Go As Planned

The good-natured support of many peers can be helpful or harmful depending on the situation. It is bad enough when the frustrating situation is a call, but when it is an internal injustice, sharing stories of when other officers got the short end of the stick can make this situation worse. The new officer might begin to think it is normal for officers to be overlooked, underappreciated, or even worse, taken advantage of. Here is a situation designed to demonstrate this principle.

Officers in an agency find out that a desirable specialty assignment will soon open. Those who are in charge encourage all officers to put forth their best effort because work performance is one of the main components considered when selecting an individual for the position. Sergeants make their recommendations, officers get their paperwork together and internal jockeying for the position ensues amongst the ranks.

One officer—let's call him Officer Smith—is excited about the potential opportunity. He has always been a top performer and is well liked by his supervisors. He decides to really kick it into high gear and spends the next several months bringing his true best effort to the table. He has always been a good officer, but he is redefining professionalism and productivity with his current efforts. Officer Smith is never late. His uniform is always clean and pressed. He has met with his supervisors and asked what he can do to best prepare himself for this opportunity. He listened to open and honest feedback on his past performance, owned any mistakes and has taken corrective action to ensure those situations will never recur.

Officer Smith is a dream officer, bringing his best effort forward every moment until the position becomes available. He prepares a professional, formal memorandum of interest. He updates his training records and polishes his resume. Officer Smith even purchases a new suit for the interview. He knows he has the support of every supervisor in the agency. No one has worked harder for this opportunity. When it is his turn in the process, he gives the best interview of his life.

After the interviews, the panel moves forward with a recommendation. When it comes time to make the final selection, the chief chooses, you guessed it…not Officer Smith.

If you've spent any time working in law enforcement, you've seen some version of this. You knew what was going to happen before I told you. Maybe you knew the ending because it's your story. Maybe it is the story of a friend or of the person you like least in the department. Whether the missed opportunity was a promotion, not being selected for a specialty assignment or not being transferred to a more desirable shift, the frustration remains. It is confusing, it is aggravating, and it can be overwhelming.

There is something inherently wrong when the institution responsible for ensuring fairness and justice in society (the police) has practices within internal operations that are not fair and just. The reasons for the injustice do not matter. You can blame it on politics, favoritism, or create a million other excuses, but the result is the same. When injustice happens, it very often does not make sense to the good officers of our profession. It also doesn't make sense to the rest of us who watch it happen over and over again. When processes do not make sense, it's very difficult for any officer to learn a lesson from the experience and keep pushing forward.

We Have Options

While it may seem that nothing can make this type of injustice so frequently seen in the police profession better, there is something that can help. Possessing resiliency can take the negative psychological impact out of the disruption. Resilience, of course, does not change the outcome, but it does change the way we think about the situation. This changes our response.

Instead of responding with anger and frustration, we respond with a proactive plan for the future. We know getting stuck in the past doesn't serve us well. We refuse to ruminate. We allow ourselves a healthy amount of time to be angry with the results of the situation and then we get over it. We move past the situation, not because the outcome was acceptable, but because we refuse to be made powerless by choosing to live in the past.

True resilience results from knowing what we can and cannot control. Like character, it is developed through purposeful daily habits. It is created by understanding how we fit into the situation and the level of ownership we chose to accept. Once we understand our role, we must thoughtfully consider if we could have adapted our strategy in any way that would have more likely brought about success. If we could have made adjustments that might have changed the outcome, we know what to do next time. If not, we tried our best. No need to spend a disproportionate amount of time being angry. We must move forward.

Truth be told, there are some things that just happen. If we did not make the decision, and we had no power to influence the person who did, there is little we could have done to change the outcome. Resiliency helps us accept disappointment with grace and dignity. It helps us plan ahead for a better future. This is much more productive than allowing anger to consume us. It is also more psychologically healthy than choosing to stay stuck in the past talking about what should have been.

Resilience gives us control of our response to a situation. We know our actions matter. We find a way to harness that. Like a ship on a stormy sea, we adjust our sails and navigate the storm. We all know it is not the water in the sea that causes a boat to sink, it is the water that gets inside the hull that creates that compromise. Psychological resiliency helps us keep that destructive disruption on the outside where it belongs. The importance of developing resilience cannot be dismissed. If we can master psychological resiliency, we will be able to have the most powerful state of mind any law enforcement officer can achieve. We will become unfuckwithable.

Chapter 9: Stress and the Need for Control

*"Water in the boat is the ruin of the boat, but water under the boat is its support." - **Rumi***

- Understand how unmanaged stress is negatively impacting police officers both personally and professionally
- Explore how stress might bleed over and impact the family unit
- Understand the dynamic relationship between stress and control and how it might be causing challenges for law enforcement professionals

Matters of Control

The quote opening this chapter is one of my absolute favorites. It seems to capture the complexity of the human condition in one brief statement. The same stress that keeps us engaged and training for the ever-changing demands of our profession can be our demise if we let it get to us. This concept is so applicable to police operations you would think Rumi was talking about our profession specifically when he wrote it. We are so focused on helping other people that we often fail to help ourselves. At times we let the disruptive situations consume our mind rather than exercising mental dominion.

The stress of this profession will control you unless you learn to manage and control it. When you encounter this stress, you will almost certainly experience an adrenaline release. That will trigger the production of cortisol. Cortisol is better known as the stress hormone. Excessive cortisol in police professionals can have a myriad of negative physical and mental health implications. "The chronic exposure to human tragedy may place police officers at special risk for mental health disorders and the potential for misuse of alcohol or drugs" (Austin-Ketch, et al, 2012, p.22). This is clearly something we can no longer ignore.

High levels of cortisol are caused by chronic exposure to stressful situations. Basically, the definition of police work. Elevated cortisol levels have been associated with a wide variety of symptoms including irritability, headaches, and sleep disorders. (Dahlgren, Kecklund, & Åkerstedt, 2005). Digestive dysfunction, weight gain, and lack of mental clarity are just a few of the other effects excessive stress has on the human body. The cortisol being put into our systems as a biological response to the stress we are encountering is a natural occurrence and something we cannot control. Therefore, we must take a proactive approach to processing the cortisol out of our system.

If we know as police officers we are going to be exposed to a disproportionate number of stressful situations and the associated cortisol production, we need to be doing something about it. We need to take intentional action designed to combat this reality to ensure we do not fall victim to all the negative impacts excessive cortisol can have. We need to take action to ensure the level of stress we are exposed to as part of our profession is not compromising our ability to have a long and healthy life.

For years, I suffered from many of the symptoms of elevated cortisol. A combination of my high level of stress combined with my need to feel in control of situations was making me both physically and mentally unwell. I am so fortunate that I found a doctor who worked to identify the cause of my symptoms instead of just giving me a band aid. Stress-related illness does not have to be our reality just because we are police professionals. We have a choice to proactively manage our stress and take control of our physical and mental health.

Even though we may not be able to control the details of the situation causing our stress, we can always control our reaction. In that simple statement lies tremendous power. In learning to respond to situations beyond our control in a healthy and logical way, we regain control of ourselves. Starting to manage our stress proactively instead of reactively is the first step on our journey toward wellness.

In the entertaining and insightful 2016 book *The Subtle Art of Not Giving a F*ck: A Counterintuitive Approach to Living a Good Life*, author Mark Manson makes some astute observations on control. He takes the famous quote from Spider-Man, "with great power comes great responsibility," and flips it. He proposes that with great responsibility comes great power.

When we start owning what is happening to us, Manson contends, we have the ability to take action. It doesn't matter if the disruption is our fault—we can get in there and start fixing the damage. We are great at this when it comes to helping members of society, but when it comes to internal matters, we are far more resistant to fixing problems we did not create.

Taking this approach to a broader view, we did not cause our high level of stress, police work did. We did not create our body's instinctual stress response - that was built by design to help early humans deal with the stressors of their very different environment. Even though these things aren't our fault, we can still do something to fix them. We must take action regardless of fault to ensure we remain the masters of our fate.

Family Impact

I am fortunate enough to travel across the country and present on matters of officer health and wellness. One of my favorite groups to present to are the spouses of law enforcement officers. This group, for the most part, is incredibly interactive and brutally honest. That honesty is refreshing and helps to create meaningful conversation.

Not a single presentation to spouses passes without an in-depth conversation about the concept of control. I will often open the conversation by asking which of the audience members believe their law enforcement spouse has a control issue. Not surprisingly, almost all hands go up. Sincere and knowing laughter usually follows, as the members of the audience look around and suddenly feel much less alone in their struggles.

I then go on to explain the origin of the control issue that is obviously presenting in their homes. As police officers, we are trained to go into out-of-control situations and establish stability.

When a situation begins to spin out of control, we step in and take assertive action. If it continues to escalate and we need assistance, we call for backup. It does not matter how much reinforcement we need to call for; we work together and stabilize the situation.

At home, we enviably deal with similar dynamics. Even the most solid families have less than perfect moments. When this happens, and we attempt to handle the situation, the habits learned at work often don't serve us well. In our homes, complex family dynamics often surround us. These dynamics create situations that sometimes seem out of control, like a family argument. Often at work, we don't have the time to sit and listen to all sides. We want the conflict to stabilize as quickly as possible. As a result, instead of taking our time and working with our family members to explore solutions that serve all parties, we come up with a quick (and often temporary) fix. Our instinct is to manage the situation and provide stability, so that is exactly what we do. Our daily behaviors at work become our daily habits at home.

It's very difficult to tell the human psyche that a lack of control at work is unacceptable because it can be a threat to your safety, but a lack of control at home is a non-threatening part of a normal family dynamics. Unfortunately, the part of the brain that can understand that differentiation isn't the same part of the brain that controls our threat assessment pattern and the resulting response. This means adrenaline is released and we become more assertive. The result can harm the health of our family relationships.

Power Vs. Control

When we start taking responsibility for our wellness, we step into a place of great power. As we mentioned, as police we often encounter situations that are out of control. Or at least they seem to be that way until police intervention is offered. These situations present in a wide variety of circumstances and can look like anything from a domestic argument to civil unrest. The police show up, handle the situation, and move on to the next call.

The uncertainty of these situations and the immediate creative problem solving they require is the part of the job that attracted most of us to this profession. The desire to work in an environment where no two days are alike is one of the unique qualities police work offers that few other professions can match. Another common reason for people being attracted to police work is a strong desire to help others and make society a better place. Unless we learn to handle the chaos that presents as a normal part of our professional duties, we will be unable to help in the way that so many of us desire.

Many police officers mistakenly believe they can control chaos by attempting to direct and control other people's actions. Let me see your hands, stop, and don't speak are only a few of the verbal commands we use to control others behavior to stabilize the situation and ensure all persons are safe. Other tactics such as separating parties and containing the scene are also used as effective control efforts. These tools are necessary for any police professional to command a situation and ensure the safety of all parties involved, as well as accomplish other essential functions such as the preservation of evidence. While these efforts are necessary and effective, something more is also needed to ensure proper handling of a situation.

Self-control is often undertrained in law enforcement. This is our true source of power to control situations. The importance of working to ensure human factors (such as the fight or flight response) do not get the best of us during stressful situations cannot be understated. This was discussed in depth earlier in this book. A key component of self-control lies in self-awareness. By knowing the human body and how it is hardwired to respond to stress, we can begin to train to overcome our stress reactions and improve our officer safety and police performance. In order to effectively harness control of others, we need to always ensure we are in control of our behaviors and our emotions.

Emotional Intelligence

Emotional control is directly tied to a concept commonly referred to as emotional intelligence or EQ. Becoming proficient in emotional intelligence requires skill development in four areas: self-awareness, self-management, social awareness, and relationship management (Bradberry & Greaves, 2009). These steps are progressive with self-management not being possible until self-awareness is achieved. If you are not self-aware, you will miss the warning signs that will allow you to effectively self-manage. Subsequently, if you are not managing yourself, you will not be able to see how the social environment could potentially trigger you into undesired responses. Clearly, relationship management can only be done once you are able to manage yourself and better understand your social interactions. Emotional intelligence offers the key to both personal and professional success.

Emotional intelligence is about more than how you allow yourself to be impacted by other people and societal triggers. It is also about being aware of how your actions impact others. I am bold enough to attest the measure of social impact is magnified by anything you say or do in a police uniform. This causes emotional intelligence to be even more important for the police profession to understand.

Police are triggers for some people. Whether it is based on a bad experience, a resistance to authority, or unfair prejudice, the fact that some people just do not like the police cannot be ignored. I am aware, based on numerous conversations I have been a part of, many police professionals think this is the other person's problem and there is not much they can do if a person has adopted that as their mindset. I promise you; this is not just a problem for the other person - as law enforcement professionals, this is a problem for all of us.

When someone is triggered, they become agitated by almost everything that is said and done after the triggering event occurs. If they are triggered by the police, that means everything we do, no matter how reasonable, will get them even more upset. Officer safety always needs to be paramount in situations such as these. That being said, emotional intelligence may offer some insight on how to best respond to a person triggered by police presence.

When a person is in an agitated emotional state, reasoning with them can be difficult. As we discussed earlier, the emotional brain is in control and the logic system is difficult to re-engage. As police, we need to ensure the other individuals agitated state does not influence our emotional state. Emotions can be contagious if not managed appropriately. We saw this recently in the COVID-19 pandemic in spring of 2020. People were suddenly stockpiling toilet paper and the grocery store shelves were empty. COVID did not even cause digestive upset! People were afraid of the uncertainty of the times ahead and began making emotional, fear-based decisions. The ability for another human being's emotional state to affect our own is real and something we need to be aware of and consider in our efforts to best serve the public.

Developing emotional intelligence not only allows us to see how other people impact our emotional state, but also allows us to examine how our emotions and behaviors impact others. This is very powerful in police operations. Anyone who has spent any time in police work has met that officer who shows up on a call and causes the "stuff" to hit the fan. You know the guy - things are calmed down, everyone is going their separate way for the evening, then "that guy" shows up as back-up. It is as if he has emotional lighter fluid that he sprays all over the situation with his mere presence. Now, people are re-agitated, two are going to jail, and you are stuck with a ten-page report. What this officer needs more than anything is to study emotional intelligence. When we as a profession start to truly understand this, we can build agencies composed of officers who are a helping force to everyone.

Just Breathe

The concept that controlling our breathing can help us control the chaos of our minds is nothing new. The response of our bodies is directly tied to the meter of our breath. Breathe rapidly and shallowly and our heart rate will rise. Slow our breathing and deepen our breaths, and our heart rate will slow in response. If we can do this purposefully when we are in a non-stressed environment, the question that begs to be asked is if we can also do this in a stressful environment once fight or flight has kicked in.

One of the fundamental concepts of the ancient practice of yoga is that stillness of the mind is necessary to achieve stillness of the body. The technique used to quiet the mind is controlled breathing. In yoga and meditation, students are taught to bring their attention to their breath to help them achieve control of their thoughts. The therapeutic benefits of both yoga and meditation on those who work in high stress professions are well researched and backed by science (Hilton et al, 2017). These practices have been proven an effective treatment for Post-Traumatic Stress Disorder (PTSD) in military personnel (Barnes, Rigg & Williams, 2013, Bergen-Cico, Possemato & Pigeon, 2014). It is time to explore if some of the fundamental concepts that are helping others working in high stress professions can be used by law enforcement to improve the health and wellness of our nation's law enforcement professionals.

At times, solutions to challenges we see in the law enforcement profession can be found in nonconventional ways. The United States Military launched programs to teach yoga and meditation after discovering the healing benefits of these practices. By training military members in these practices, they are developing skills to help them better control their breath response. Police agencies across the nation have also incorporated yoga and mindfulness practice into their training regimen. Like the military, this will develop skill to prepare the body and mind to better handle stress.

Not only is the stretching found in yoga beneficial for the body, but the mindfulness component is imperative for that crucial self-awareness piece previously discussed. Controlled breathing or tactical breathing can help change the body's response to stress, specifically in intentionally slowing the increased heart rate and rapid breathing linked to adrenaline release of flight or fight response. Once that adrenaline release occurs there are biophysical realities such as auditory exclusion and tunnel vision that might set in. Being mindful of the body's response and intentional about our efforts can help us take corrective action during these times. Controlling our breath can help minimize the impact of some of these disruptive human factors.

Mindfulness and controlled breathing techniques can help police retain emotional control and minimize the negative impact human factors can present during critical times of emergency operations. Like any other motor skill function, the training needs to take place before the emergency situation unfolds. Officers often handle high stress situations from muscle memory. This is why we train so frequently on the range. A deadly force situation is sure to trigger a stress response in an officer. It is important we have the repetitions of drawing our weapon to ensure we are able to respond to a deadly force threat appropriately.

By training controlled breathing techniques as part of standard practices, it is possible to incorporate this powerful tool into law enforcement operations. Most specifically, this training should be integrated into preparing for those types of situations where a stress reaction is likely to occur. Firearms training, defensive tactics, and emergency vehicle operations are three areas that come to mind as natural areas to incorporate tactical breathing techniques into training. By teaching controlled breathing and mindfulness during those critical trainings, we are better able to provide officers with the ability to retain emotional control during high stress encounters.

Chapter 10: Hope for the Future

"I am the master of my fate. I am the captain of my soul."
- **William Ernest Henley**

- Learn how to create personal change with massive intentional action
- Understand how small changes can lead to big results
- Learn to identify psychological injury through symptoms of disruption

Rise to the Challenge

With all the challenges discussed thus far, it is clear that the stress we encounter during the course of our profession is creating both physical and mental health challenges for police professionals across the country. While some of us can continue with the commitment to physical fitness and mental preparedness we started our profession with, others become unintentionally compromised somewhere along the way. For many of us this is a pendulum effect where we swing between times of commitment to fitness and wellness and times of utter exhaustion where we cannot find the energy for self-care.

Knowing the stress and critical incident exposure we see as a part of our professional experience may be creating many of the major problems our police officers face, we now have the power to develop solutions. These solutions will not only serve police officers working on the streets today, but also for future generations of law enforcement officers. It is our professional duty to take action to create a healthier policing culture for generations to come.

By examining the research, we can start understanding what is happening in the law enforcement culture that might be compromising our physical health and mental wellness. The truth of the matter cannot be ignored. Police are at a greater risk for cardiovascular disease, metabolic syndrome, and obesity than the standard population (Zimmerman, 2012). We are also at a higher risk for depression, addiction, and suicide (Heyman, 2018). How did this happen in a profession that tests for both physical fitness and mental stability prior to hiring? And more than that, what can we do to change it moving forward?

An Apple a Day

We must get serious about taking better care of our health. Heart disease is not only the number one killer in America, but also the number one cause of death in law enforcement professionals. Hypertension and coronary artery disease increase your chances of a deadly cardiac event, on or off duty. This is true for all of us, even those police professionals who seem to be in exceptional physical shape to the outside observer. True health is not always something that can be easily seen from the outside. While a healthy BMI is important, more telling is what your bloodwork says about what is happening behind the scenes.

Routine physical health screenings are a required part of assessing health. A healthy cholesterol level is a far better indicator of cardiovascular risk than a low body fat percentage. Unlike the size of your biceps or waist, cholesterol levels cannot be seen with the naked eye. Blood work screening, usually offered as part of an annual wellness exam, is the only way to know if you are at risk before an event happens. Knowing your levels allows for proactive intervention (usually medication or lifestyle adjustments) instead of sitting around waiting for a cardiac event to occur.

    We all know that healthy person committed to fitness who had a heart attack one morning while out for his or her daily run. Outside of a rare genetic condition, the warning signs of a problem were probably there for that individual to see in their blood... if they had only gotten the screening. If we could just get members of our profession to go to the doctor for wellness exams regularly, we would be able to better understand our risks and take preventative action.

    There has never been a time that holistic health has been more important than now. With the pandemic scare of 2020, the true threat of underlying health issues and compromised immune systems came to the forefront of our national health crisis. The only way to know if you have a potential underlying health issue it to go to the doctor regularly for wellness screenings. When the world was on lock-down, we all still had to go to work. We must stay healthy. Our lives depend on it.

    Today, almost all insurance companies provide no-cost annual wellness visits. This is because the medical industry knows if they catch a problem early most issues are highly treatable, or even reversible, with the correct intervention. Despite this, many police are still reluctant to go to the doctor for their annual wellness check-up and bloodwork. If you are amongst this stubborn group, please do yourself a favor and call and make an appointment with your doctor now.

If we understand how the mindset of our culture is contributing to our compromised wellness, we can come together and take action to change it. Make a commitment today to go to your annual wellness appointments. Go and ask the person you love the most to keep you accountable for doing so. We are far more likely to follow through with a commitment when we share our intentions with someone we love.

When you get to your appointment, talk to your doctor about the importance of getting regular bloodwork done to ensure your own personal health. This simple test is almost always covered by insurance and is the best way to see the early warning signs of cardiac disease. Ask your doctor about a cardiac calcium screening. Even if insurance does not cover this test, it is often highly affordable, and the results might save your life. Please do not be that guy or gal who we lose to a heart attack a few months before you were supposed to retire. What you don't know can hurt you. Take action and be informed. Knowledge is power.

In addition to annual wellness screenings with your doctor, there are several other things you can to do ensure you are part of the solution to create a healthier police profession. While regular medical visits are amongst the most important, these other factors can also greatly increase the likelihood that you have the best chance to remain healthy in an arguably unhealthy profession.

What Man Destroys; Nature Heals

Nature can heal the damage created by man and by modern society. While this is not specific to police, law enforcement can definitely benefit by remembering the therapeutic effects of being out in nature. The health and wellness benefits of the great outdoors are widely known. In fact, many mental health professionals regularly "prescribe" time outdoors to clients struggling with issues such as depression and anxiety.

Whether you call it Vitamin N, Nature Therapy, or something else entirely, connecting with nature has great benefits including improved

mood, reduced stress and the ability to lower blood pressure (White, et al, 2019). The course of action is simple: step outside and unplug. Whether you are walking or jogging, hiking or biking, climbing a tree or taking a nap, the benefits are the same. Pick your preferred activity and soak in the sunshine and fresh air. When you do this, it is almost impossible to look around at the great big world and not realize there is something bigger than you. Once this is realized, your problems and frustrations are almost sure to feel a little less significant in the grand scheme of things.

Medical doctors and psychological professionals alike agree on the benefits of getting out into nature. Movements such as Park Rx, a joint effort between the Golden Gate National Park Conservancy and the National Park Service, shows how clinicians, public health bodies, and health-minded community professionals are working together to make open spaces accessible to all Americans. While exercising outdoors would provide the ultimate health benefit, even something as simple as going to a park and sitting on a bench will help. The next time you feel like you need to sit around and do nothing, try doing it outside to allow the healing forces of nature to start to work on your body and mind.

For those of you who might be skeptics, I would like to propose a question to you - imagine riding in a car or riding in a convertible- which is more invigorating? In both situations, you are taking automotive transportation from point A to point B, but they are entirely different experiences. Why is that? The answer, of course, is because of fresh air and sunshine. Getting outdoors and exposed to the elements causes a biochemical reaction in our bodies. Our systems release serotonin when we are exposed to the sun. It is normal, natural and powerful. It will boost your immune system and put you in a better mood without requiring effort other than stepping outdoors.

Our Actions Matter

Other initiatives such as the Blue Zones (Buettner, 2012) take a more holistic approach to health and wellness. While nature exposure, social factors, and community support are discussed as major components to discovering longevity, the impact of diet and an active lifestyle are recognized as the key findings of the book. Other books, such as *The China Study* (Campbell & Campbell, 2005) and the more recent contribution *How Not to Die* (Gregor & Stone, 2018) have studied the impact of diet and nutrition on health and reached the same conclusion. While all these books have different approaches to their research, they all basically say the same thing - the daily choices we make have a great deal of impact on our physical health.

In fact, lifestyle factors, including diet, have been shown to play a more significant role than genetics in determining longevity and propensity for disease. The research is fascinating. Take a look at Japan, who was for many years without a fast-food industry. During this time obesity was almost unheard of and both heart disease and cancer rates were very low. Once fast food was introduced, the areas having access to these restaurants saw a significant increase in the prevalence of obesity and disease. This is not coincidental, but the correlation may be more complicated than you think.

Research clearly shows a calorie restricted diet has tremendous health advantages (Furman, 2018; Sinclair, LaPlante & Delphia, 2019). It is likely much of the obesity and disease was related to a shift from a calorie restricted diet to an excessive calorie diet rather than any one ingredient in fast food. Fast food is commonly calorie dense due to the amounts of preservatives added during the processing of the food product. While this allows for a longer shelf life, it packs on non-nutritionally dense calories, often seen as an increase in fats and oils.

The calorie density in fast food can cause people to be overfed (too many calories for their activity level) while being left undernourished (not enough micronutrients in the food they are eating).
Think about the food choices police often make while working in a high-stress, shift- based environment. The men and women working in our profession are experiencing the same phenomenon as Japan experienced once fast-food arrived on their island.

We need to take our commitment to caring for our nutrition as seriously as we take our commitment to caring for our physical health. Comprehensive care of both these areas require long term strategy as well as daily time and attention. It is amazing to me that many police officers are more selective of the fuel they put in their personal vehicles than the food they put in their own bodies. This is an area we have to get more serious about.

When I was working midnights, I could not find a healthy food option while on the street to save my life. It just was not available. This meant if something happened, and I showed up to work without a lunch, I was either not eating or eating complete junk. Foolishly in my youth, I thought eating something was better than eating nothing. Because of this misunderstanding, many nights I found myself in a fast-food drive through. The research on calorie restricted diets and disease clearly prove my assumption to be incorrect. Twenty pounds and a significant loss of energy later, I finally learned to load my duty bag with healthy snacks.

Today it is a different world. Even the smallest gas station often offer healthy food options. For a quick snack that will satisfy your hunger while offering nutritional density reach for fresh or dried fruits, veggies or even a bag of nuts. Avoid highly processed foods at all costs. One of my favorite rules to follow is if your grandmother wouldn't be able to recognize every item on the ingredient list, you should probably not be eating it.

Learning to Identify Psychological Injury

There is no doubt the amount of traumatic incident exposure being seen during a law enforcement career is compromising the psychological wellness of our police professionals. The good news is we know there are ways to proactively manage this and the other areas causing law enforcement stress. By incorporating many of the things previously discussed into our daily habits, we can lessen the potential for that stress to have long lasting negative impact. Unfortunately, many of us have been working for years without this information and stress has already taken hold. If this is your situation, this section is for you.

The body is a miracle machine. It is literally designed to repair damage done to it, but we must create the right environment for that healing to take place. We also need to be able to recognize when we have encountered a situation that has created a wound. As stated before, this is true for injuries to both the body and the mind. This is so simple with our physical bodies. When the damage is done, we can see it with our eyes or feel it through physical pain. We know where the injury is, and we likely know what caused the injury. We can take corrective action and get on with the healing process.

The damage or injury that may be caused to our psyche does not present with the same obvious indicators. You cannot see the injury with your eyes, and the pain caused may be masked as anger, avoidance, or other subtle symptoms. Recurring thoughts, disturbing dreams, and emotional responses to a past situation are some of the ways our mind communicates that our brains need to heal. If we are not taught those signs are an indication of injury, we may fail to respond with healing intervention. Avoidance and rumination can also be signs our brain is struggling to make sense of something that happened. There is no more shame in experiencing any of these symptoms than there is in getting a bruise after being punched in the eye.

Most of us were not taught what to expect when our psyche takes a hit. As a result, we fail to identify a psychological injury when it occurs. Our profession tells us it is crucial to our survival to train on how to address wounds to the body. Buddy rescue and tactical trauma trainings teach us all how to take immediate action to protect ourselves and others from physical injuries that occur on the job. To not do so could put us at great risk for harm. I think we can all agree this training is some of the most important training we get. This is the training designed to provide us with the skill to deliver intervention in the field that just might save our lives.

When it comes to matters of the mind, however, we often do not feel the same compulsion to act. In the moment, chances are we don't even know something disruptive happened. We have not received training on signs of injury or intervention techniques. Even worse, many law enforcement officers feel there is a negative stigma associated with suffering from this type of wound. This results in an almost universal approach to addressing psychological distress; we ignore it, we hide it and we deny it. This strategy is killing us. As a profession, we deserve better. We must train to identify and respond to these injuries proactively.

When a psychological injury occurs, the importance of taking action is equally as important as it is when there is a bodily wound. Failing to address it immediately will only allow the injury to get worse. Often the signs of psychological injury (rumination, sleep disturbances, or continued anger) are there. If we know to watch for them, we will see them, but these signs are less visible to the outside observer. We need to start educating officers on how to identify the potential warning signs of psychological injury and train them on what the appropriate intervention is.

Rumination and anger are like mental energy bleeds of the mind. If you do not control that energy loss, you are slowly losing your life force. That will compromise your ability to lead a healthy life. Left unaddressed, it will also compromise your professional performance. We need to take action to address the psychological injury the same way we would if a physical injury occurred.

Like surface injuries to the body, some injuries to the mind require little to no attention to repair. For a small matter, something as simple as writing the required police report or discussing the call with a co-worker might provide all the healing that you need. Other issues, more serious or a culmination of events, may require more intervention. Let me explain why small matters may repair themselves without us even noticing.

The Minds Ability to Heal

Language is regulated in the same part of the brain as logic and reasoning. Because of this, either talking or writing about something has significant therapeutic effects. This is the premise talk therapy was built on - you repeatedly apply language to the concerning situation and soon it has been resolved. This is also why journaling is such a popular self-help intervention. This is because when you attach language to an emotion-based situation, it helps your brain move the experience out of the emotional processing center (the most internal part-the lizard brain) to the pre-frontal cortex (the most external part of the brain-higher order human functioning). Once language is applied to the situation, logic is also applied. This allows us to regulate our emotional reaction and heal from the psychological bruise.

There is no way to predict the amount of impact any single event will have on your psyche. Additionally, what does or does not cause psychological upset says absolutely nothing about your ability to do this job, your mental strength or your intelligence. Situations with a more significant psychological impact will differ by individual but might involve violent actions, horrific details, or events that hit close to home because of a personal connection. Cumulative events, or repeated exposure, may cause an otherwise insignificant event to have a larger impact. For those situations that are more traumatic, writing your report or speaking to your co-worker one time might not be enough.

Repeated conversations might be necessary to process the negative psychological impact of the disturbing event. This will fully move that experience from that place in our brain where it continues to be processed as an emotional experience to the place in our brain where logic and reason can be applied.

Our brain then allows us to store the situation as a memory. This is what healthy psychological processing looks like.

To think, for all these years I have held resentment against that old-school Sergeant who used to mark up my written reports in red pen and make me rewrite them. I now realize by repeating those writings, he might have helped me process some of the more gruesome crime scenes that otherwise would have left a lasting wound on my psyche (I wonder if he knew he was having that impact or if he was just an ass?). The repetitive process of expressing the situation in written word was the psychological equivalent of several sessions of talk therapy. I guess I owe him a thank you!

Chapter 11: Impossible to Unknow

"The future depends on what you do today."

— *Mahatma Gandhi*

- Understand advancements in the field of psychology that can help police process trauma
- Learn to harness your personal power and make decisions designed to direct your life
- Learn strategy to stay strong and committed to our profession during challenging times

EMDR and the Psychological Revolution

When those larger, psychologically upsetting events occur, sometimes we must have repeated conversations or language applications to fully process all the complex and disturbing details. This is not only associated with gruesome scenes, but it can also be associated with the internal politics of police operations. Missed promotions and other injustices have the ability to hit our psyche in a significant way and cause psychological damage. If we just walk around carrying our frustration and disappointment inside, the psychological wound festers instead of heals. We get weaker instead of stronger. If this is allowed to continue, serious problems can occur.

As a rule, police do not like discussing things that upset them. They would rather stay upset and angry than become vulnerable and discuss their "feelings". This is one of the many contributing factors creating the stigma against receiving psychological services in our profession. Eye Movement

Desensitization Reprocessing (EMDR) is the psychological intervention that is likely to change the way law enforcement approaches mental health.

EMDR is an intervention that allows for processing of the disturbing psychological event without the need to discuss how the incident made the officer "feel". EMDR is said to resolve in six sessions what talk therapy used to take six years to address. The advent of this technique was uncovered by Dr. Francine Shapiro and is documented in her book *Getting Past Your Past* (2012). The best part about this book is that Dr. Shapiro not only discusses how she discovered the technique, but she goes into detail on how it works. This book has a self-help section where Dr. Shapiro tells us how we can use these techniques for self-care in the event we are feeling stuck on a situation. Of course, we can also go to a trained practitioner to expedite the healing process.

To better explain Dr. Shapiro's technique, we only need to revisit some concepts presented earlier in this book. We already discussed how emotionally charged or traumatic situations can get stuck in the emotional processing center of your brain. We also discussed how applying language to these situations can help move the experience from where it is stuck (in the emotional processing center) and still being experienced in present time, to where it belongs (in your memory). Dr. Shapiro has discovered how to use bilateral brain stimulation (touch, auditory stimulation and/or eye movements) to bypass the language process and force the memory out of the emotional processing center. This brings the situation directly to the part of your brain responsible for memory, logic and reasoning.

When a disturbing experience is moved from the emotional processing center to the memory center of the brain, it loses its disruptive power. The result of this intervention is that you now own the memory, the memory no longer owns you. For years, I worked in a holistic counseling center with many EMDR trained practitioners. The results they were seeing with their clients were amazing. I even became trained myself to better understand the applicability of this technique. During this training, I saw the power of this intervention firsthand. Through the years I have spoken with hundreds of officers who have used EMDR successfully. EMDR can help police grow past their post-traumatic stress and recover from the psychological damage caused by the many stressors of this profession.

If you are an officer who still has one of those calls that makes you feel that tightening in your throat, please do yourself and your family a favor - find an EMDR practitioner in your area and allow this amazing intervention to help you heal. If that is not something you are open to, please purchase the book and try to help yourself. Anything is better than doing nothing. If you don't like to read, there is an audio version of the book available. However, you choose to approach this, it is time for action. Stop making excuses. Break free from the hauntings of your past. A healthier happier future awaits! You just have to go out and get it.

Post-Traumatic Growth

It is possible to achieve a state of personal growth after a traumatic event, but first you must ensure that event has been processed by your psyche in a healthy way. As we just discussed, EMDR can help get you there. Once you arrive, the exciting ability to experience personal growth is open to you.

The secret to post-traumatic growth was the surprising finding in the research done and documented by Dr. Brene Brown in her bestselling books (2010, 2012). As Dr. Brown researched shame, she learned of the intense hardships her research participants had lived through, and in understanding their psychological resiliency, she made a shocking discovery. It was vulnerability that made these people strong - their willingness to admit to their flaws and have an honest discussion about them. The ability to openly discuss their personal failures and the challenges they faced created within these individuals a great strength.

Police work is a profession that has a low tolerance for imperfection. This causes many of us to fake our way through less than perfect times and pretend everything is fine. When we do that, we rob ourselves of the opportunity for true post-traumatic growth. This is where we admit we are not perfect. We are willing to see the situations from a variety of perspectives to ensure we have a depth of understanding, and when it is time to move forward, we have not only "learned a lesson" but we have grown stronger from the experience.

Post-traumatic growth is the most beautiful part of resilience. It allows a person to make a choice about how the heavy experiences of their past impact and shape their future. Will the disruptive events that have been endured become weights or wings? This powerful choice lies with each individual.

The last chapter opened with the last line of the famous poem Invictus (1875). This line speaks directly to the opportunity for post-traumatic growth. When something terrible happens, we have a very important choice to make. We can remain a victim and use the situation as an excuse, or we can become a survivor and rise above our circumstance to create a better and brighter future. In this choice lies our true power. Each of us are the master of our fate. We are the Captain of our souls. Nothing can hold us back as long as we chose wisely.

Historically, police work has had a reputation for being unfair when it comes to internal happenings. Some officers get away with things that would cause others to face discipline. Hard working officers are overlooked while do-nothing officers get promoted (remember Officer Smith). This focus on situations that are not fair or balanced is in direct conflict to a person's ability to grow after a traumatic event. Each of us as individuals get to decide if we are going to dwell on the injustices of the past or if we are going to focus on the promise of a better future. That decision determines if we experience post-traumatic growth or get stuck in a victim mindset.

When faced with this situation, we find ourselves having to stop looking at solving the larger problems of the profession as a whole and start focusing on owning our personal experience. Ownership does not mean we need to accept something unfair as fair; it means we need to accept it as reality. It is an event that already occurred; no matter how unjust it may have been. Once we accept this reality we can decide if we are going to remain stuck or if we are going to choose to move forward. As individuals, we can overcome even the most difficult challenges facing our profession, but we need to make an intentional decision to do so. Once that is done, we are well positioned to find the courage to move forward without looking back. Part of this process may be exploring any ownership of the situation.

The Power of Ownership

Extreme ownership is a concept brought to mainstream attention in the book of the same title written by members of the Navy SEALs (Willink & Babin, 2015). In this popular leadership book and podcast, the authors advocate for taking responsibility for events, even when they are not your fault. When you own an event that has happened in your reality, you give yourself the power to fix the situation. Conversely if you sit around blaming others, you remain powerless and a victim of circumstance. This has wide applicability in police work, not only for matters of creating resiliency, but also in dealing with larger issues.

Corruption is something that has plagued the police profession for over a century. While some argue the onset of police corruption was during the prohibition, others believe police were abusing their power and authority long before those days. I say this not to upset any of the noble men and women working in our profession today, but to make the point that from an occupational perspective, admitting our imperfections and using them as ways to grow are not exactly our strong suit.

The presence of this corruption has led to a great mistrust between police and some segments of our society. I am not talking about justifiable police action that is misinterpreted, I am taking about the infrequent but present inexcusable behavior we have seen from members of our profession. For too long we have blamed corruption and incidents of excessive use of force on a "few bad apples". As recent times have seen an uprising in civil unrest, this concept may prove to hold the keys to healing strained relationships. Remember what Mark Manson said, "with great responsibility comes great power".

Like Jocko and Leif in *Extreme Ownership,* Manson discusses how taking responsibility is different than owning fault. He proposes it is only possible for people to fix a situation when they are willing to take responsibility for what happened. Where this gets complicated, is when we realize with responsibility comes obligation, and with obligation, vulnerability. If we own it, we must be able to do something to fix it. Excuses are completely removed.

Every man and woman who has chosen police work as their career knew the history associated with this profession. You and I entered this noble profession intending to make it better. We did not cause the problems plaguing our profession, but if we are willing own the problems, we might be able to help solve them. If we know there is a way we can actually help make things better, don't we have a responsibility to take action? And if so, why aren't we doing it? Enter vulnerability. Admitting we are part of an imperfect profession somehow makes us feel less safe. This creates real challenges.

Feeling vulnerable is not something police do well. In fact, most of our training is intended to ensure we are ***not*** vulnerable in times of compromised safety. It is difficult to tell people that it is ok to feel vulnerable in some situations but not ok in other situations. When we feel vulnerable, we have an instinct to protect ourselves. This often manifests with us defending ourselves and our profession. When we are defensive, rarely are we problem solving.

We have to decide who is it we want to be. We must commit to being a defender of justice if we are going to serve as police. We must commit to defending justice even if the source of the injustice comes from within our own profession. Are we willing to own the misgivings of our profession, or are we going to continue to blame the proverbial few bad apples? This is a choice we have to make.

Policing in Times of Chaos and Disorder

As I write this section, the world is in a chaotic state. Protests and riots are breaking out across America in response to police misuse of force. Hell, protests and riots are also breaking out across America in response to appropriate police use of force. Some people are making a very vocal statement that they hate the police. Calls for defunding are being heard throughout the nation. These are incredibly challenging times.

Police went from being heroes who were putting their lives on the line during the COVID Pandemic to being the enemy almost overnight. As this happened, there remain over 900,000 police officers in America who did not do anything wrong but are still a target of this hatred and rage. There are protests and riots. Lives are being lost and violence is being perpetrated in the name of justice. As I watch what is happening in the world, it is sometimes difficult to believe it is real. As all this is happening, these same 900,000 plus officers who did nothing to deserve this backlash, have to protect their communities, innocent people and businesses, and themselves from crowds seeking to cause destruction.

Situations like this cause a whole new level of stress for modern day law enforcement. This situation also shows the importance and exigency for the need for real officer safety solutions. While this book speaks to some universal approaches that might be applied to larger issues, it is more designed to give each individual officer the tools they need to take care of their mental and physical health in these incredibly trying times. If each of us makes a commitment to prioritize our personal health and mental wellness, the profession as a whole will become healthier as a result.

As we move thought this complex profession, each of us will be presented with many challenges over the course of our careers. It is up to each of us to rise to those challenges and use them as opportunities for growth. We must stop allowing vulnerability to put us into defense mode and trying to explain situations that do not make sense. We must stand tall and remember the reason we took the oath. This is our profession and we must take it back.

There may be moments when we may have to defend our profession. There is a difference between the defensiveness of ego-driven denial and standing tall and proud in defense of what we believe in. When are called to take a stand, I hope none of us lose sight of where we can find ownership. In each of these situations the opportunity for growth will be inherent. In taking ownership we will be able to better serve society as we move into the future.

We can no longer stand back and say, "I did not cause this problem, why are you blaming me?" We must stand together and say, "We see what has happened and we are committed to fixing it." We must heal this crippling divide. The best way for us to do that is for each of us to remain healthy, strong and committed during these extremely challenging times.

Spirituality

It would be irresponsible to offer a book about wellness without discussing the concept of spiritual health. This is because officer wellness is truly holistic in its construct. To fully be prepared to meet the challenges of this profession will require strength of the body, mind and spirit. The fortitude it takes to remain strong through the current storm is much easier with some help from above.

Wellness occurs in the individual as part of the whole system. It does little good to be physically fit but mentally unsound. Likewise, it can be compromising (especially from an ethical perspective) to be psychologically healthy but spiritually lost. To have a strong spiritual sense of purpose but to have a physical body that is not well enough to meet the demands of the profession would also leave the officer in a compromised state of safety. The goal is to be healthy and whole.

A lack of spiritual health can result in us feeling a deep sense of unhappiness. In part, this unhappiness may be created by losing your ability to understand your role in the larger picture of things. Without spirituality, it is more difficult to keep perspective during challenging times. This can compromise our ability to remain grateful, despite the challenges or devastation at hand. An attitude of gratitude is one of the essential components of happiness (Acher, 2010). Random acts of kindness are also effective in helping remind you to not only scan the world for good, but to help put good back into the world.

All these things are more easily achieved with a belief in a higher power. Spirituality, religion, faith, call it what you want, but recognizing that we, as humans, are part of a larger plan is an essential part of connecting to and maintaining our sense of self-worth.

This sense of self is especially important for police. We are constantly exposed to the most negative elements of life. We are condemned for crimes we did not commit, and our integrity is attacked due to the uniform we chose to wear. These realities are even more reasons spiritual health is an essential component of our overall wellness. When injustices like this happen, we must know who we are to stay the course. Having faith in a higher power can help us stay true to ourselves when things start to feel out of control.

My intention here is not to tell anyone what to believe in - that choice belongs to each individual officer. That being said, I am suggesting each of us would be well served to believe in something bigger than ourselves. For without that higher power, it can be difficult to find the greater meaning in life. Without a moral code, it will be more difficult to keep our character from becoming compromised. If we are to stay true to our profession, we must understand who we are and be willing to fight the good fight. A spiritual foundation can help us remain diligent in that pursuit.

Chapter 12: Tying it all Together

"You are what you do, not what you say you do."

– *Carl Jung*

- Learn to apply intentional action to improve your quality of life
- Understand how stress is compromising your ability to thrive
- Learn to create work life balance without sacrificing your commitment to your profession

Start with You

The officer wellness revolution is above all things a call to action. It is a challenge to each and every law enforcement officer to take responsibility for their personal health and happiness. I am asking you to stop making excuses and start taking corrective action. We can have a healthier profession! For that to occur, we all have to take responsibility and commit to making better choices for ourselves.

I have attempted to combine academic research with personal experience to explain what is happening in the heads and hearts of America's law enforcement officers. The stress of this profession combined with unhealthy habits are compromising our quality of life. It does not have to be this way. We have the power to change it.

I have demonstrated how accepted psychological phenomenon may be impacting law enforcement professionals negatively. The intent of this is to empower the men and women in uniform to understand the stress of their professional experience is real and must no longer be ignored. I have worked to explain how the action steps presented in selective chapters in this book can be followed to help each and every police officer achieve a healthier, happier career. A happier, healthier life!

Take Control of Your Health

Every man and woman who rises to the challenge to become a law enforcement officer is both physically and mentally healthy at the onset of their professional career. The concepts presented in this book shows every one of us that we have the power to stay that way despite the challenges of our professional experiences. We will all see terrible things, some more than others. Crazy amounts of internal bullshit will happen, over and over again. For the entirety of our career, we will bathe in the negative elements of society. These are our realities, but they do not have to compromise our mental or physical health.

This book is intended to help our current law enforcement officers overcome the physical and psychological challenges that have been ignored by our profession for far too long. It is no coincidence that police officers from different communities in very different parts of our country suffer the same higher rates of depression, addiction, and divorce. This book offers solutions to address the unacceptable levels of chronic illness seen in police officers by showing officers how to build a foundation of healthy daily habits. It empowers officers to make informed choices that will result in a greater level of wellness. This book presents research to help us all understand what might be contributing to the high suicide rates seen in our profession and finally do something to stop it. This book has been written to save lives.

The concepts are very simple. We must recognize how our current behaviors contribute to negative consequences. We must then apply intentional action and change the behaviors that are not serving us well. If we have been complaining; we need to quit bitching and take action. If we have been a victim of bad circumstance; we need to own the situation and create a brighter future. If we have become physically unfit; we need to go to the doctor, have our bloodwork checked and re-commit to a healthy lifestyle including a responsible exercise routine. If stress has been making us miserable; we should introduce intentional actions designed to proactively reduce our levels of stress. If we keep doing the same thing, we will keep getting the same results. If we want things to change, we have to be willing to do something differently. This book has provided a different approach.

Overcoming Exhaustion

Earlier in the book, I explained how psychological exhaustion manifests in the body the same as physical exhaustion. This means if you are stressed out, you will not have the mental or physical energy required to create a good life. This is why we find ourselves sitting on the couch doing nothing during the majority of time after work.

Arguments were also presented on the need to actively combat this exhaustion by making a commitment to movement. Take a cold shower, take a walk or get to the gym. Do something to show your mind that you are asserting your will into the situation. The time for law enforcement to be too exhausted to create a happy life outside of work is over. Start living the life you have always imagined by applying the action steps discussed in this book.

Build intentional enjoyable activities into your schedule. We cannot wait to see how we "feel" after work. We will likely feel depleted. We need to rise above that and start to engage in our lives in a bigger way. No more opting out of events because we don't want to deal with other people. We need to jump in with both feet. If we get there and we are truly miserable we can always leave. Imagine how our loved ones will respond when they realize we are back to the fun-loving people we used to be. We have been gone too long my friend. It is time we get in there and LIVE.

Work Life Balance

My doctoral dissertation revolved around the topic of work life balance. This involved several years of intensive research combined with in depth interviews and assessments of the incredible people who agreed to participate in my study, to whom I am eternally grateful. One of the things I learned during this process is that law enforcement professionals struggle with work life balance in a very different way than the rest of society.

Law enforcement professionals tend to put the needs of other people before our own. Even worse, we tend to put the needs of our agencies over the needs of our family. I am not talking about the emergency call out situation. We all understand the obligation to that. I am talking about the small ways we spend our time, energy and focus on the agency when we should be paying attention to the people we love.

Our loved ones have been taking a back seat for too long and it is having a terrible impact on our ability to retain healthy relationships. Our divorce rate is through the roof (last I heard it was at 86%), and these broken relationships are tied to our high levels of depression and addiction. Again, if we want things to change, we have to take different action.

It is the nature of the beast in police work that sometimes our job will interfere with our personal life. We will get called in, our days off will get shifted around and we might even be forced to unexpectedly switch shifts. We all have experienced Murphy's Law in some form or another. If you don't believe me, make dinner plans after work next week. I can almost guarantee the night you make plans you get a late call that interferes with the dinner. This is to be expected. It is part of our burden.

When it happens, there is an effective strategy to handling it; own it, apologize, and make up for it. That goes something like this, "Honey, I'm sorry I caught that late call and had to cancel dinner plans. It disappointed me as much as it did you. The situation was totally out of my control. I know this job is sometimes hard on the both of us... maybe you more than me. Let me make it up to you. Next week, I will take you to your favorite restaurant on my day off. That way we can be sure nothing gets in the way of us having a nice night together. How does that sound?" Simple, straight forward and sincere. Then, and this is important, follow through and do it!

Sometimes our work will interfere with our life. We must accept that. This next part is the key to work/life balance for police. *Sometimes our lives need to interfere with our work.*

Yes, you heard me correctly. There are times our personal lives should take priority over our professional responsibilities. Strategically and intentionally we have to start making this happen. I am not talking about blowing anything off. I am talking about purposeful, planned decision making. An example may be if your kiddo has an important ball game, or there is a family wedding you need to attend. If you think you can work shift and be off in time, you are taking a huge gamble. Don't chance it. There is a better way.

This is what our vacation days and personal time is for. Not to work overtime... to have time away from work to create a good life. On special occasions, we need to learn to take off a few hours early to ensure we don't catch that inevitable late call. Maybe we need to learn to take the whole day off and live like a normal person. Please try it. I am willing to bet your family will love you for it. This is the only way you will be able to find the sense of balance you have been looking for.

We are still not going to be able to make each and every social event. We need to be honest about this with our loved ones and establish some ground rules. Our job will still get in the way of some things, but it doesn't have to get in the way of everything. Together we can find a balance that works for us and those we love. For too long we have been completely responsive to the needs of our profession and far less responsive to the needs of our family. Through open honest communication and purposeful action, we can create work life balance that works for us.

Implementation

This book has presented a great deal of information on how we, as police, can create healthier lives for ourselves. The recommendations are a combination of research and lived experience of not only the author, but countless others who have shared the traditional law enforcement struggle. We no longer have to accept that law enforcement is an unhealthy profession tied to chronic disease and early death. We can be the change!

Within these pages, action steps each officer can implement to create an immediate positive change have been presented for consideration. Now is the time for us to put these healthy habits into practice. While each chapter offers several areas an officer can make meaningful changes, the following list is provided for those readers wondering where to start:

- Chapter 1: Identify and replace unhealthy habits to improve overall health
- Chapter 2: Find a way to get more sleep, unplug frequently or incorporate other ways to relax
- Chapter 3: Make time investments in your personal relationships
- Chapter 4: Learn to ask for help with little things
- Chapter 5: Create a list of proactive strategies you can use to help manage stress
- Chapter 6: Motivate yourself to exercise regularly to create a healthy body and mind
- Chapter 7: Identify and take action to move towards the best version of yourself
- Chapter 8: Unlock your personal power by adjusting your attitude and mindset
- Chapter 9: Find ways to protect your family from your work stress
- Chapter 10: Go to the Doctor and get a wellness check up
- Chapter 11: Identify situations from the past that are still bothering you and work them out
- Chapter 12: Create work life balance by making a commitment to prioritizing your family

References

Achor, S. (2010). *The happiness advantage: The seven principles of positive psychology that fuel success and performance at work.*

Amlani, N.M., Munir, F. (2014). Does Physical Activity Have an Impact on Sickness Absence? A Review. *Sports Med* **44**, 887–907 https://doi.org/10.1007/s40279-014-0171-0

Austin-Ketch, T.L., Violanti, J., Fekedulegn, D., Andrew, M.E., Burchfield, C,M. & Hartley, T.A. (2012) Addictions and the Criminal Justice System, What Happens on the Other Side? Posttraumatic Stress Symptoms and Cortisol Measures in a Police Cohort, *Journal of Addictions Nursing,* 23:1, 22-29, DOI: 10.3109/10884602.2011.645255

Barnes, V.A., Rigg, J.R, Williams, J.J., (July, 2013) Clinical Case Series: Treatment of PTSD With Transcendental Meditation in Active Duty Military Personnel, *Military Medicine*, Volume 178, Issue 7, Pages e836–e840, https://doi.org/10.7205/MILMED-D-12-00426

Bergen-Cico, D., Possemato, K., & Pigeon, W. (2014). Reductions in Cortisol Associated With Primary Care Brief Mindfulness Program for Veterans With PTSD. *Medical Care,* 52(12), S25-S31. doi:10.2307/26417876

Bradberry, T., Greaves, J., & Lencioni, P. (2009). *Emotional intelligence 2.0.*

Brown, B. (2012). *The power of vulnerability: Teachings on authenticity, connection, & courage.*

Brown, B. (2010). *The gifts of imperfection: Let go of who you think you're supposed to be and embrace who you are.*

Buettner, D. (2012). *The blue zones: 9 lessons for living longer from the people who've lived the longest* (2nd ed.). Washington, D.C.: National Geographic.

Campbell, T. C., & Campbell, T. M. (2005). *The China study: The most comprehensive study of nutrition ever conducted and the startling implications for diet, weight loss and long-term health.* Dallas, Tex: BenBella Books.

Center for Disease Control and Prevention (2020). https://www.cdc.gov/nchs/fastats/suicide.htm

Dahlgren, A., Kecklund, G., & Åkerstedt, T. (2005). Different levels of work-related stress and the effects on sleep, fatigue and cortisol. *Scandinavian Journal of Work, Environment & Health, 31*(4), 277-285. Retrieved May 28, 2020, from www.jstor.org/stable/40967503

Davis, T. (July, 2015). Wellness initiatives assist in boosting employee morals. *American Psychiatric Association Newsletter* https://www.apa.org/pi/about/newsletter/2015/07/employee-morale

Fuhrman J. (2018). The Hidden Dangers of Fast and Processed Food. *American journal of lifestyle medicine*, *12*(5), 375–381. https://doi.org/10.1177/1559827618766483

Greger, M., & Stone, G. (2018). *How not to die: Discover the foods scientifically proven to prevent and reverse disease.*

Gu, J. K., Charles, L. E., Burchfiel, C. M., Fekedulegn, D., Sarkisian, K., Andrew, M. E., Ma, C., & Violanti, J. M. (2012). Long work hours and adiposity among police officers in a US northeast city. *Journal of occupational and environmental medicine*, *54*(11), 1374–1381. https://doi.org/10.1097/JOM.0b013e31825f2bea

Hegberg, N. J., Hayes, J. P., & Hayes, S. M. (2019). Exercise Intervention in PTSD: A Narrative Review and Rationale for Implementation. *Frontiers in psychiatry*, *10*, 133. doi:10.3389/fpsyt.2019.00133

Heyman, Mariam. (2018). Study: Police Officers and Firefighters Are More Likely to Die by Suicide Than in Line of Duty. Retrieved on 11th September 2019 from. Study: Police Officers and Firefighters Are More Likely to Die by Suicide Than in Line of Duty. Retrieved on 2nd September 2020 from https://issuu.com/rudermanfoundation/docs/first_responder_white_paper_final_ac270d530f8bfb Hilton, L., Maher, A. R., Colaiaco, B., Apaydin, E., Sorbero, M. E., Booth, M., Shanman, R. M., & Hempel, S. (2017). Meditation for posttraumatic stress: Systematic review and metaanalysis. *Psychological Trauma:*

Theory, Research, Practice, and Policy, 9(4), 453–60.
https://doi.org/10.1037/tra0000180

Joiner, T. (2005). *Why people die by suicide.* Harvard University Press.

Kulbarsh, P. (March 13, 2018). Law enforcement and Heart Disease. Officer.com

Manson, M. (2016). The subtle art of not giving a fuck: A counterintuitive approach to living a good life.

Robbins, M. (2017). *The 5 second rule: Transform your life, work, and confidence with everyday courage.* Brentwood: Savio republic.

Rusch, H. L., Rosario, M., Levison, L. M., Olivera, A., Livingston, W. S., Wu, T., & Gill, J. M. (2019). The effect of mindfulness meditation on sleep quality: a systematic review and meta-analysis of randomized controlled trials. *Annals of the New York Academy of Sciences, 1445*(1), 5–16.
https://doi.org/10.1111/nyas.13996

Shapiro, F. (2012). *Getting past your past: Take control of your life with self-help techniques from EMDR therapy.* Emmaus, Pa: Rodale Books.

Sinclair, D., LaPlante, M. D., & Delphia, C. (2019). *Lifespan: Why we age--and why we don't have to.*

Stevens, J.E. (3 Oct, 2012) *The adverse childhood experiences study: The largest study you never heard of began in an obesity clinic.* ACE's Too High News.
https://acestoohigh.com/2012/10/03/the-adverse-childhood-

experiences-study-the-largestmost-important-public-health-study-you-never-heard-of-began-in-an-obesity-clinic/

White, M.P., Alcock, I., Grellier, J. *et al.* Spending at least 120 minutes a week in nature is associated with good health and wellbeing. *Sci Rep* **9,** 7730 (2019). https://doi.org/10.1038/s41598-019-44097-3

Willink, J., & Babin, L. (2015). *Extreme ownership: How U.S. Navy SEALs lead and win.*

Zimmerman, Franklin H. MD Cardiovascular Disease and Risk Factors in Law Enforcement Personnel: A Comprehensive Review, Cardiology in Review: July/August 2012 - Volume 20 - Issue 4 - p 159-166 doi: 10.1097/CRD.0b013e318248d631

About the Author

Chief Laura LV King is a generational police officer who has served the law enforcement profession since 1996. She holds a doctorate in psychology and actively works to improve police operations though an increased understanding of the principles of psychology. She's a professional speaker and trainer on mental wellness and psychological resiliency for police organizations throughout the country. She holds several certifications in fitness, nutrition and weight management and continues to work one on one with clients as a certified life-coach. She is trained in EMDR and is on a self-proclaimed mission to heal the police profession.

Laura King is a graduate of both Northwestern University's School of Police Staff and Command and of Session 265 of the FBI's National Academy. In addition to her personal experience in law enforcement. King has spent years researching mental wellness for law enforcement professionals. Her research has proven mental wellness is not "soft stuff"... for police it is a matter of life and death.

This book is an offering on the most pertinent information she has discovered in both her research and her lived experience. It is designed to help law enforcement stay healthy and safe over the course of their careers.

"This is information every officer must know to survive their career. It is no longer enough that we go home at the end of our shift. We deserve to go home healthy, happy, and well-adjusted."
 -Dr. Laura LV King

Read more at https://www.mentaldominion.com/.